The Church of Scotland
Four Years' Course for Bible Classes
Volume Two

THE LIFE AND TEACHING OF JESUS CHRIST

THE LIFE AND TEACHING
OF JESUS CHRIST

by the Very Rev. Professor
JAMES S. STEWART, D.D.

*The Church of Scotland Committee
on the Religious Instruction of Youth*

Published by
The Church of Scotland Committee on Youth
121 George Street, Edinburgh 2
and printed in Scotland by
Robert Cunningham and Sons Ltd., Alva

First Edition 1933

Reprinted 1933, 1935, 1936, 1937, 1941, 1942,
1945, 1947, 1948, 1949, 1952, 1954

Second Edition 1957

Reprinted 1961, 1965

TO

MY WIFE

CONTENTS

ABOUT THE USE
OF THIS COURSE

The Purpose of a Bible Class

In the religious education of young people, the period after they leave Sunday School, at the age of fourteen or fifteen, is one of peculiar opportunities and peculiar dangers, and a great deal depends on what the Church attempts to do for its young people at that point. It is here that the Bible Class ought to come in with a four years' programme, and it is of the greatest importance that this should be regarded as the next stage, after Sunday School, of a religious discipline which goes on without a break as the normal training for communicant membership of the Church. In some churches that four years' period will be provided for in a series of graded Bible Classes under different teachers: in other churches the minister will take all the young people through that period in one comprehensive class. This will depend on local circumstances, partly on numbers. The important matter is that the continuity should be maintained, and that the minister should keep in close touch. If the young people are graded into classes under different teachers, it is important that the whole should be regarded as a unified Bible Class Department, and should meet together under the minister for the devotional part of their hour. Further, it is of the greatest importance that these four years should be devoted to really vital Christian education, so as to prepare young people for a Church membership which will have both zeal and knowledge.

The Four Years' Course

The present series of text-books is intended to help teachers in that matter. The attempt has been made to divide the main ground of essential Christian instruction into a four

years' programme, as follows: I. The Preparation for Christ
in the Old Testament; II. The Life and Teaching of Jesus
Christ; III. The Story of the Church (from the Apostles to
the present day); IV. Christian Faith and Practice (embracing
a treatment of Christian belief, the Christian Sacraments and
Christian conduct). The four text-books on these subjects are
not to be regarded as progressively graded in the above
order. In those classes where all the adolescents are grouped
together for the whole four years, such graded teaching is
impossible, as different members of the class will receive the
successive subjects in a different order, according to the year
in which they join the class. Moreover, it is hoped that the
text-books will be found useful in classes of a different type
from either of the above, such as the Boys' Brigade Bible
Class. Thus the attempt has been made to prepare the books
in such a way that the teachers can adapt the lessons to the
needs of their own classes, which is what a good teacher
must in any case do.

How to use the books

These text-books are, of course, for the use of the teachers,
not the pupils. It hardly needs to be said that even for a very
inexperienced teacher the method of reading the lesson aloud
out of the book to the class is a hopeless one. The effective
teaching of a Bible Class requires a much more exacting preparation on the teacher's part. The lessons in these books
contain not only the main body of the material, but also,
here and there, suggestions to the teacher as to illustrative
matter and practical applications, as well as occasional references to other useful literature. In the case of Text-book No. I,
there is also a small teachers' booklet (price 1s. 6d.), which is
meant to help teachers to adapt the material to the less ad-
vanced classes. In the case of all four text-books, there is
published a corresponding booklet for the use of the pupils
(price 1s.), and it is important that full use should be made
of this. Among other things, it contains a daily Scripture
lectionary, the passages for the days of each week being
chosen so as to lead up to the lesson on the Sunday. It is

very well worth while to do all in one's power to encourage the young people to use this lectionary. Not only does it make it much easier to do good teaching in the class, but it initiates the young people into the habit of reading the Bible daily for themselves through those four years of their adolescence.

The most important thing of all is that the teacher should regard the Bible Class as a religious discipline, in which the young people are consciously led on into Christian discipleship, and so into whole-hearted and intelligent membership of the Church of Christ. Thus the four years' course will be linked up with the Young Communicants' Class. This does not mean that the young people should be discouraged from entering into full communion until the whole four years have passed. The whole course indeed ought to be regarded as, in a sense, a continuous Young Communicants' Class, so that at any point it might be natural for young people to feel that they wished to 'come forward' for communicant membership. But above all, the aim is not merely to produce Church members, but to produce good men and women—to help the young people through the critical and difficult years of their adolescence in such a way that they will emerge as genuinely Christian men and women with a faith of their own. In those years they need all the help that the Church can give them; and what better work can the Church ever do? It is worthy of all the trouble that we can take, all the care and skill, enthusiasm and devotion, that we can bring to the task.

1: THE GOSPEL RECORDS

Mon. John i, 1-14   The Word made Flesh
Tues. Heb. ii, 1-9   Seeing Jesus
Wed. Eph. iv, 1-16   The Work of an Evangelist
Thur. Matt. ix, 9-13
         Matthew, the Tax-gatherer-Evangelist
Fri. Acts. xv, 35-41   John Mark, who made good
Sat. 2 Tim. iv, 10-11; Luke i, 1-4
         Luke, Doctor and Missionary
Sun. John xiii, 23-26; xxi, 20-25
         The Beloved Disciple

Psalm xix, 7-10: 'God's law is perfect'
Hymnary 196: 'Come, Holy Ghost, our hearts inspire'

1. *The Making of the Gospels*

Jesus wrote no autobiography. He left nothing in writing at all. He committed Himself and His teaching simply to the hearts and memories of the men who knew and loved Him. And they did not fail Him. The four little books that we call Gospels are our primary, and practically our only, sources of information about the life and the words that have changed the world. We may wish the story had been told with greater fulness and detail; but we know that, short as it is, it is enough. It has given Christ to every race and age.

Strictly speaking, the Gospels are not biographies at all. The earthly life of Jesus covered more than thirty years, yet you can read these little books at a sitting. Long periods of Jesus' life are passed over in complete silence. If everything were told, says John, 'the world itself could not contain the books that should be written' (John xxi, 25). What we have is a set of 'memoirs', selected historical reminiscences. But it is a selection with a purpose. 'These are written that ye might believe that Jesus is the Christ, the Son of God; and

I

that, believing, ye might have life through His name' (John xx, 31). Each of the Evangelists aims at giving a portrait of the Master. And each writes inevitably from his own angle. Hence we have really four distinct portraits of Jesus. That is vitally important for us today, for Jesus is ever so much bigger and more wonderful than any one man's view of Him could possibly be. But while each portrait has its own distinctive features, they are all the same Jesus, with 'the light of the knowledge of the glory of God' upon His face.

At a later time, other 'Gospels' made their appearance; but these are rightly excluded from the New Testament, for in them fact and legend were inextricably mingled. Certain 'unwritten sayings of Jesus' (i.e. sayings not recorded in the Gospels) have also come to light, but the authenticity of these is doubtful. Famous amongst them are the following: 'Let not him who seeks cease until he finds, and when he finds he shall be astonished, astonished he shall reign, and having reigned he shall rest.' 'Raise the stone, and there thou shalt find Me; cleave the wood, and there am I.' 'Whoso is near Me is near the fire.'

The earliest of our four Gospels appeared probably between the years 65 and 70, that is to say, some thirty-five to forty years after the earthly ministry of Jesus had closed. Why was that long interval allowed to elapse? Nowadays when a great man dies, his friends would not dream of allowing a whole generation and more to pass before publishing his 'Life': were not the Evangelists unpardonably dilatory about their obvious duty? No, it was not dilatoriness. Probably one reason for the delay was that they, and indeed all the early Church, were so busy evangelizing the world, so absorbed in their active service, so convinced that the King's business required haste, that literary work of any kind was crowded out. Nor must we forget that the bulk of these early Christians were living in expectation of a speedy end of the age (had not Jesus Himself said, 'The kingdom of heaven is at hand,' and again, 'This generation shall not pass till all these things be fulfilled'?), an expectation that made the writing of books a superfluity. Moreover, the continued presence of the risen, exalted Christ with His followers was so vivid and so real to many of them that they may not have felt at first the need to be continually going back to what Jesus had said and done in the days of His flesh. Hence the days grew into months, and the months into years, and a generation had gone before the first of our Gospels appeared.

No doubt fragmentary accounts of isolated sayings and deeds of Jesus were in existence before the Evangelists wrote. St. Luke, for example, in the opening verses of his Gospel tells us that he had a large quantity of such miscellaneous materials to sift out and to draw upon in constructing his own narrative. Here a parable would have been preserved in writing, there the story of a miracle, there a group of sayings, there a body of teaching on some special subject, the Sabbath, or fasting, or prayer. To that extent the Evangelists found the way prepared. These verses (Luke i, 1-4) should be carefully read and studied. They are of extreme importance for determining what Biblical 'inspiration' means, and what it does not mean. Luke there makes it perfectly clear that the inspired writers were not miraculously freed from the necessity of hard historical research which other writers have to face. Inspiration was not God magically transcending human minds and faculties: it was God expressing His will through the dedication of human minds and faculties. It does not supersede the sacred writer's own personality and make him God's machine: it reinforces his personality and makes him God's living witness.

When at last the impulse to write down the story of Jesus began to make itself powerfully felt, various motives contributed to it. For one thing, the expectation of a sudden end of the world had by this time receded, and with the lengthening of the years and the gradual passing of the men and women who had known Jesus and been eye-witnesses of His life and death and resurrection, it became obvious that to continue to rely on oral tradition and on fragmentary documents would be extremely precarious. The Evangelists felt a call to save the story of Jesus for unborn generations. Moreover, there were the needs of the thousands of young

converts from paganism to be considered. A young man
joining the Christian Church in the generation after Christ
would naturally want to know what the Lord's Supper meant
and how it had originated: obviously the most helpful thing
to do would be to put into his hands some authoritative
narrative of the events in the upper room on the night of
Jesus' betrayal. Again, there was the danger of heresy to be
combated. When divergent views on central matters of faith
appeared within the Church, the question inevitably rose.
What had Jesus actually said about this? What had He
taught? Once again, when the Church was attacked from
without, and false, damaging representations of the character
and conduct and motives of its members were being circu-
lated far and wide, what better defence could there be than
simply to hold up before the eyes of the world the story of
the Master who had given the Church its being, the Master
they were pledged to serve? Along these different lines the
need for preserving the sacred story in some definite and
permanent form was growingly felt; and the Evangelists set
to work.

2. *The Earliest Gospel*

St. Mark's Gospel was the first to appear. Now there is a
very ancient and reliable tradition (it is from Papias, one of
the earliest of Christian writers, that it comes) which tells us
that 'Mark became the interpreter of Peter', and that he
'wrote down accurately everything that he remembered'
from Peter's discourses and sermons. That is of the utmost
importance. It gives us a picture of young John Mark accom-
panying the great Apostle on his preaching tours, standing
in the market-place while Peter preached to the crowds, and
helping Peter to deal with inquirers when the meeting was
over. We see Mark listening again and again to the story of
the life and death of Jesus as it came from Peter's lips, until
he knew that story by heart himself, and was living in the
atmosphere of it; and when at last death claimed his great
friend and leader, and Mark was left alone, he wrote the
story down. And so the earliest Gospel was given to the

world. It is a great thing to know that behind it stands the witness of Peter, one of the Master's most intimate friends. Hence its historical authority is beyond dispute.

The words, 'The Gospel according to St. Mark', which stand in our Authorized Version at the beginning of this little book, are a later addition. Mark himself gave no name. The Evangelists were not seeking literary reputation. Their passion for the glory of Christ had submerged every thought of self. They were not concerned that the world should know from whose hands the story had come. It is in keeping with this, too, that they tell the story with the utmost frankness and candour, never seeking to present the disciple-band in a specially favourable light, or to minimize their blunderings and faults. Mark's Gospel, as we have seen, is really Peter's story: Peter has certainly not tried to save himself! 'He rebuked Peter, saying, Get thee behind me, Satan' (viii, 33); 'they all forsook Him and fled' (xiv, 50); the story of Peter's denial (xiv, 66 ff)—it is all here, with nothing hidden, nothing palliated. Earthly fame was nothing to these men: the beauty of Christ was everything.

But if Mark is silent about himself, we can gather a good deal about him from other parts of the New Testament. The following passages in Acts should be consulted: xii, 12 (which provides us with the interesting suggestion that Mark's home may have been the home of 'the upper room' and the Last Supper, in which case Mark himself may well have been an eye-witness of Jesus); xii, 25; xiii, 13; xv, 36 ff; also the following references in the Epistles: Col. iv, 10; 2 Tim. iv, 11; Philemon 24; 1 Peter v, 13. Mention should be made of one exceptionally attractive and fascinating suggestion, namely, that within the Gospel itself at one point (Mark xiv, 51 f) there is a veiled reference to the writer. Who was this 'certain young man' who appears so mysteriously in Gethsemane? Only Mark of the four Evangelists records the incident. Nor can Peter be his authority here: Peter had already fled (xiv, 50). The story must have come from the 'young man' himself. And there would have been no point in recording it, unless he had been someone fairly prominent

in the early Church of subsequent days. May not the nameless figure in Gethsemane have been Mark himself? It is impossible, of course, to settle the matter definitely; but at
least the identification seems not improbable.

3. The Gospel for Jewish Christians

When we turn from Mark's little book of 'memoirs of Jesus'
to that of Matthew, one difference strikes us at once. Mark's
principal interest is in the events of Jesus' life: Matthew
concentrates rather on His teaching. Another early Christian
tradition (again from Papias) tells us that 'Matthew wrote
down the sayings of Jesus in Hebrew, and each interpreted
these as best he could'. It seems that Matthew the disciple
had a diary in which he entered from time to time the conversations and the teaching of his Master, and this diary
added to Mark's narrative became the basis of the Gospel
that now bears his name. It is specially a Gospel for Jewish
Christians. Note in this connexion the frequency of Old
Testament quotations, the importance attached to the Mosaic
law, and the emphasis on the Jewish Messianic hope and its
fulfilment in Jesus. With the modesty which, as we have
already seen, characterizes all the Evangelists, Matthew tells
the story of his own conversion in a single verse (ix, 9). Nor
is any effort made to conceal the depths from which Christ
had lifted him: he was a tax-gatherer, 'sitting at the receipt
of custom', a man, that is to say, socially ostracized, for he
had sold country and conscience, and probably character,
too, in a profession which in the eyes of every loyal Jew was
branded as dishonourable. In what unlikely places Christ
finds His evangelists and ambassadors!

4. The Gospel for Gentile Christians

St. Luke is the one Evangelist who was not a Jew. He used
both Mark and the Sayings-Source which appears in
Matthew, but he had other materials as well. His Gentile
birth and sympathies account for what is by far the most
striking feature of his Gospel, namely, that it is a *missionary*
Gospel, and that the Christ it portrays is not primarily

the Messiah of Israel at all but the Saviour of the whole earth. The very fact that the book is dedicated to Theophilus— possibly a high official under the Roman Government, and not yet a Christian—is significant. Notice, too, that at the very outset Luke lifts the story he is going to tell out of a purely local, Palestinian setting and deliberately places it in the framework of world history: not only does he trace the genealogy of Jesus right back to Adam as the founder of the race (contrast Matthew, who begins with Abraham, the founder of Israel), but he connects the coming of Jesus with world events (see, e.g., iii, 1). Moreover, the missionary motive was obviously for Luke the deciding factor in determining which incidents and parables, out of all the mass of materials at his disposal, he should include in his published memoirs of Jesus. In this connexion it is only necessary to mention the Parable of the Good Samaritan, the incident of the one grateful leper (xvii, 11, 'and he was a Samaritan'), such sayings of Jesus as, 'They shall come from the east, and from the west, and from the north, and from the south, and shall sit down in the Kingdom of God' (xiii, 29), and above all, the Parable of the Prodigal Son, a story which carries a national as well as an individual reference, the younger son standing for the Gentile world and the elder for the Jewish. It is pre-eminently the Gospel of a universal hope.

Luke himself, who wrote the Acts of the Apostles, as well as the third Gospel (see Acts i, 1), was a physician (Col. iv, 14). It may well have been in his capacity as doctor that he was first introduced to Paul, whose travelling companion he subsequently became; and we can readily understand how valuable Luke's professional skill must have been to the great Christian missionary, whose physical health was at the best precarious (2 Cor. xii, 7 ff), and who had frequent experience of wounds and scars and bruises in his Master's service (2 Cor, xi. 25 ff; Gal. vi, 17; Acts xiv, 19). Luke's training as a doctor also accounts for the special place given in the Gospels to the healing miracles of Jesus, and for the occurrence throughout his narrative of certain technical

terms which were used in the medical language of his day.
Sir William Ramsay has made the very attractive suggestion
that Luke hailed originally from Philippi, though he was
now resident in Asia Minor, where Paul had first met him
and converted him to Christianity; and that when Paul in his
dream at Troas saw 'a man of Macedonia' beckoning them
to 'come over and help' (Acts xvi, 9), it was his friend Luke
whom he saw. It would be entirely congruous with the whole
spirit of the third Gospel, and with its passionate missionary
interest, that its author should have been instrumental in
bringing Christianity across to the western world.

5. *The Last Gospel*

When we pass from the first three Gospels (often called,
because of their common viewpoint, the 'Synoptics') to the
fourth, we feel at once that we are in a different atmosphere.
From the earliest times this difference was felt, and the words
that Clement of Alexandria quotes from a still older writer
describe it well—'John, perceiving that the bodily facts had
been set forth in the other Gospels, composed a spiritual
Gospel.' Clearly the author presupposes a knowledge of the
other Gospels in his readers, and he sets himself to supplement their narratives, and with the aid of his own spiritual
genius and mysticism to elucidate the deeper meaning of the
person and work of Jesus. It was the last of the Gospels to
appear, and the long thought and brooding and spiritual
communion of a lifetime have gone into its composition.

Among many things distinguishing this Gospel from its
predecessors, the following may be mentioned. It gives us
no parables. It concentrates on the Judean ministry of Jesus,
to the almost entire exclusion of the ministry in Galilee. It
records a whole new series of private conversations of Jesus
with individuals, notably with Nathanael, with Nicodemus,
with the woman of Samaria. It omits certain scenes where
the human side of our Lord's nature is stressed, notably the
temptation in the desert, the agony in the garden, and the cry
of dereliction from the Cross. It stresses the eternal aspects
of Christ's person and work. It gives us, not the Carpenter

of Nazareth, but 'the Word that was in the beginning with God'.

It is not likely that the Gospel in its present form is the work of John the Apostle. Other hands have worked over it (see, e.g., xix, 35; xxi, 24). But behind it we are justified in tracing the figure of the great Apostle; and the view can be strongly supported that this wonderful Gospel, in some ways the most wonderful of them all, was built up partly from reminiscences written down by 'the disciple whom Jesus loved', perhaps in the form of a diary (cf. Matthew above), shortly after the events themselves, and partly from historical sermons on the life of Jesus preached by him subsequently in Ephesus. Certainty on these matters will perhaps never be attained. What does matter is that the fourth Gospel, in setting out to supplement the other three, has gloriously achieved its purpose, and more than achieved it. It has made our picture of Jesus the Son of God full and perfect and complete.

So much, then, for our records. It is on these four little books that all our study of the Life and Teaching of Jesus must be based. And let us remember that they give us three things. They give us History. Here we have a solid bedrock of historic fact, fixed and impregnable. But they give us something more than History: they give us Revelation. For as we turn the pages, it is God's voice that we hear, God's face that we see. But they give us more than History and Revelation: they give us a Challenge. Every page renews the challenge, every line drives it home. And the challenge is— 'What *think* ye of Christ?' That first, and then—'What shall I *do* with Christ?' And the challenge haunts us till we answer.

Note to Teacher.—At the beginning of this course on the Life and Teaching of Christ, it is very important that the teacher should urge upon the members of the class the necessity of going direct to their New Testaments. No books about the Gospels can be of any value apart from a constant reference to the Gospels themselves. Class-members should therefore be asked to make full use of the Lectionaries supplied. It is on a right use of these that everything in the course will depend.

2: THE FULNESS OF THE TIME

Mon. Job xxiii, 1-10   The Cry of the Human Heart
Tues. Psalm cx.   The Expectation of a Redeemer
Wed. Isaiah xl, 1-11   The Way Prepared
Thur. Joel ii, 21-32   The Vision of Messiah's Age
Fri. John vi, 33-51   The World's Hunger
Sat. Rom. vii, 14-25 Man's Perpetual Need of Christ
Sun. Rev. vi, 9-11   How long, O Lord?

Paraphrase xxxix: 'Hark, the glad sound'
Hymnary 150: 'Come, Thou long-expected Jesus'

1. *A World Prepared*

In the Church of the Holy Sepulchre in Jerusalem, one spot is pointed out to travellers as being the centre of the world. It is a strange and rather fantastic claim. Yet there is a sense in which the corner of the earth's surface called Palestine is the geographical centre. Take the three great continents of Europe, Asia, and Africa: in between them, linking them up, lies this little land-bridge on the eastern shores of the Mediterranean. Clearly, if you were to start a movement whose aim was to extend out into the three great continents simultaneously, that neck of land would be a natural starting-point. The old legend about the centre of the world is, therefore, truer than the men who invented it realized. It was no haphazard that made Bethlehem and Nazareth and Calvary the cradle of the Christian faith. It was the best possible place for the launching of a world-religion.

But if the place God chose was ideal for the coming of the Christ, the time God chose was ideal too; and it is this we are now to consider. It was when the fulness of the time was come, says Paul, that God sent forth His Son (Gal. iv, 4). That is to say, it was when world conditions were exactly ripe for it that God's supreme revelation in history came. It was when all the factors—social, economic, moral, religious —had converged upon Him that the Man of God's right hand came forth.

> Now, God be thanked Who has matched us with His hour
> And caught our youth, and wakened us from sleeping.

So sang Rupert Brooke. And never did it happen more gloriously than when Jesus came forth from the bosom of God. The hour and the Man had met.

Search the pages of history up and down, and in all the tale of the centuries you will not find any generation in which Christ could better have come than just the generation in which He did come. 'There is a tide', says Shakespeare, 'in the affairs of men.' We can go beyond that and say that there is a tide in the affairs of God: and it is when that tide reaches the flood, when all the preparatory work is done and world conditions are clamouring for it and human souls are open, it is then, at the flood-tide hour of history, that God launches His new adventure. So it was when Luther sent his Ein' feste Burg ringing and singing along the roads of Europe. So it was when Scotland heard the rugged voice of John Knox. So it was when Wesley kindled a great fire in England. So it was supremely when upon the whole Graeco-Roman world there burst suddenly out of Galilee, with the shouts of saints and the trumpetings of angels, the sound of a new name, the name of Jesus. It was the fulness of the time, said Paul—it was the hour foreordained in the divine wisdom —when God sent forth His Son. Jesus came at the very point in history at which all the conditions were ripe for His coming.

The practical value of this study of world conditions at the birth of Christ lies in the discovery that modern conditions are closely parallel. It is the growing conviction, the considered judgement of men who can read the signs of the times that once again in world relations—social, economic, moral, and religious—God's flood-tide is coming, and that our generation is seeing what men saw twenty centuries ago, the lines of preparation beginning to converge, beginning to point to a new day of the power of the Son of Man. Today, as then, God is matching the hour with the Christ, and there is an opportunity now, unprecedented for nineteen hundred years, for Christ's evangel to get a lasting grip. For Jesus and for men the fulness of the time draws nigh.

2. *The Political Preparation*

Let us look now at some of the converging lines of preparation that made things ripe for Jesus when first He came.

We begin with this. *When Jesus came, it was the fulness of the time politically.* What was the dominating feature of the political situation of the generation to which Christ came? It was the unification of the world. That was Caesar's achievement. The day of closed frontiers was over. The day of separate, self-sufficient, antagonistic nations, gazing suspiciously at one another across bristling defences, was done. All the way from the Atlantic to the Caspian, from Britain to the Nile, from Hadrian's Wall to the Euphrates, the Roman standards could be seen. Everywhere the barriers were down. The chaos had been welded and consolidated into a community. The world was one big neighbourhood.

Three factors contributed to this situation into which the Gospel of Christ was born. One was *the Roman Peace*. If Christ had come a century earlier, His Gospel would have been blocked at every turn, blocked on the land by closed national frontiers, blocked on the ocean by the pirates who made the high seas impassable. Or if He had come a few centuries later, He would have found civilization too pre-occupied with its terrible struggle against the barbarian hordes from the north to have any ear for the Gospel. But Christ came to a generation when the Roman Peace held the world, held it no doubt with an iron hand, but held it sure and far-flung and unbroken; and men could hear the Bethlehem angels sing.

A second factor making for the unity of the world when Jesus came was *the great Roads*. From end to end of the Empire the great highways ran, triumphs of Roman engineering.

And the ten thousand labourers who had toiled on the making of the roads in the sweat of their brows little thought they were preparing a way for the Son of God. But they were. Along these Imperial lines of communication, built to carry Caesar's legions to every corner of his dominions, the missionaries of the Gospel came marching; and everywhere their message spread like wildfire. Christ's men could never have evangelized the world as they did if it had not been for the Roman Roads.

The third factor making for world unity when Jesus came was *Language*. Imagine what would have happened if the first missionaries had had barriers of language to contend with. Their advance would have been slowed down and terribly retarded, in many places brought to a standstill, and that at a stage in their great adventure when it was absolutely vital to lose no time. But as it was, wherever they went, they found there was one language that carried them through. For while each province still had its own tongue or dialect, everywhere the people were bilingual and all knew Greek. In the heights of Galatia as much as on the streets of Athens, in Spain as in Rome, the missionaries could speak Greek knowing that they would be understood. The Roman Peace, the great Roads, the common Language—these were the things that had linked the world up into one big neighbourhood, and so had prepared the way for Christ.

Compare the present day. Is history not repeating itself? The big fact that is revolutionizing the life of all the peoples of the earth today is this, that the world in these last years has shrunk amazingly, that the ends of the earth have been brought far closer together than ever they were before, that our contacts with our brother-men have been multiplied almost bewilderingly. Nothing of importance can happen in any corner of the world without being known and discussed by people on the other side of the world next morning. And the great thing about the new contacts is that they are not merely physical and mechanical contacts: they are moral and spiritual. Start a new idea in Britain or in Russia or in India, and ere long the new idea has put a girdle round the earth. It is not only words that fly faster and farther today than ever before: the thoughts of men's hearts are doing it too. What a chance for Jesus, and what a responsibility for the Church of Jesus! Only let one nation, one Church, one congregation, one soul begin to burn for Christ, and in less time than it takes to tell the heather might be on fire for Christ across all the earth. Only let one little body of Christ's people anywhere, here in our own land, if God will, feel the urgency of a new Pentecost, the inward power of the Lord Jesus, and it might not be long until on the other side of the world they were taking the Kingdom of Heaven by storm. 'Behold, I have set before thee an open door' (Rev. iii, 8). In God's grace it is wide open today, and the fulness of the time is nigh.

3. *The Economic Preparation*

When Jesus first came, it was the fulness of the time, not only politically, but also economically. Deep down beneath the shining culture of that old world, down beneath its luxury and magnificence, unrest was seething and poverty walked in rags. Two men of every three on the streets of Rome were slaves, mere goods and chattels; and sometimes the slave heart rebelled. And when the great poets of Rome sang of the Golden Age, it was generally to the past that they turned their eyes. Not for them, as for the Hebrew prophets, did the Age of Gold lie in front, shining in a happy, beckoning future; the Golden Age of plenty lay behind them, and it was the Age of Iron now.

Indeed, in many quarters of Caesar's dominions, the economic situation had reached the point of crisis when Jesus came. So it was in Palestine. The disastrous aftermath of war, the wild colossal extravagance of Herod the Great, the burden of taxation, both civil and religious, the growing over-population which made it impossible for the land to provide food enough for its own inhabitants—these things had precipitated a period of unexampled depression among the great bulk of the people. Life had grown care-ridden and full of worry. Anxiety for the morrow was written deep upon men's faces and on their hearts; and all the world seemed tangled and gone wrong. It was then, at the blackest hour, that a Voice of hope rang out in Galilee; and men's hearts leapt up and listened, for the fulness of the time had come.

Here is a question worth discussion. Do revivals of religion come more easily in times of economic prosperity or in times of economic depression? No doubt men may grow so desperately worried and care-ridden about material things, about the question of where tomorrow's bread is going to come from, that they may have little or no heart or interest left for religion. But no doubt, also, man's extremity is still God's opportunity; and the very breakdown of all human resources may prepare the world at last to listen to Christ. Certain it is that it has been out of some of the most depressed and desperate human situations that the great historic revivals have burst, like the break of a new day (see, e.g., Welch, *The Preparation for Christ in the Old Testament*, Lessons III and XIX). And who can say but that all our own distresses have been preparing for a new coming of the living Christ into human history, and making straight through the desert a highway for our God? Economically, no less than politically, the fulness of the time has come.

4. *The Moral Preparation*

When Jesus first came, it was the fulness of the time morally. Swinburne in one of his poems cries out protestingly that after Christ the world has never known the same light-heartedness again; that Jesus has taken all its natural gaiety and good spirits away; that until then the Graeco-Roman world had been perfectly happy and innocent and contented in its Nature-worship, its worship of Zeus and Dionysus and Aphrodite, that Jesus really spoilt everything.

Thou hast conquer'd, O pale Galilean; the world has grown grey from Thy breath.

But all that is false to the facts. Historically, it is nonsense. The idea of an ancient world happy and innocent and light-hearted and morally at peace is simply a myth. If you want

the real truth about that world you will get it, not in Swinburne, but in St. Paul, in that terrible picture that stands for
ever for all future ages to read in Paul's first chapter to the
Romans—a world that was sunk in moral hopelessness. 'The
world was growing old,' says Mommsen, 'and not even
Caesar could make it young again.' No, indeed; for it had
sinned its youth away, and all the freshness of the dew of
youth was gone, and only the worm, the canker, and the
grief were left. Everywhere the best spirits were in despair.
Everywhere to the noblest souls it seemed that the whole
world was pursuing its riotous way down to disaster and
oblivion and ultimate night. And it was then Christ came,
travelling in the greatness of His strength, and made the old
world new.

   May we not say that some such impact of the Spirit of
Christ upon the moral life of men and nations is one of the
prime needs of today? When the experiment of slackening
morality and tampering with codes of honour has been
carried to a certain point, inevitably there comes a reaction.
Inevitably that something of God which lurks beneath the
surface of men's hearts stands up and records its protest. The
glamour of the sensationalist creed and the lure of the modern
gospel of uncontrol have the living Christ to reckon with.
Men will not be satisfied with the ethics of the dust always.
They are growingly rebellious against them now. In the
moral sphere, the fulness of the time has come.

5. *The Religious Preparation*

When Jesus first came, it was in the fulness of the time religiously.
The old gods of Rome were either dead or dying. To fill the
gap, two expedients were tried. On the one hand, a whole
new batch of gods was imported from the East, outlandish,
Oriental deities brought in to stir Rome's jaded senses—till
amongst the philosophers the overcrowding of Olympus,
where the gods were supposed to dwell, became a standing
joke. On the other hand, the strange phenomenon of Caesar-
worship appeared: the Emperor himself was accorded divine
honours. But all expedients failed. What was a whole Pan-

theon of gods worth if they had nothing to say to a man with a broken heart? What could the divinity of Caesar say to a soul stabbed with the remorse of sin? When everything had been done that could be done, the hungry hearts of men were hungry still.

But there was something more definite than that. There was a strange sense of something impending from the side of God. In many parts of the world, men of deeper nature and more spiritual vision were peering into the darkness for some faint flush of dawn. Amongst the Jews themselves the hope of the Messiah was blazing more clearly than it had done for centuries. The great mass of Jewish literature from the period between the Old Testament and the New Testament is full of this great hope. And when any new voice rang out across the land, the voice of a John the Baptist, for instance, immediately on every lip there rose the question—'Is this the Messiah now?' The air was tense with expectation. And the Jews, penetrating as they did into every corner of the Empire, took that great dream with them and handed it on. Nothing cleared the way for Christ more definitely than that passionate hope. The fulness of the time had come.

Today, in the religious sphere, the same spirit is at work. On the one hand, just as in the Roman Empire, the old gods are dead or dying. The gods of convention, the gods of outworn, second-hand religious tradition, the gods of materialism and secularism are losing grip. And on the other hand, our generation is marked by a sudden new outbreak of interest in Jesus. Witness the books about Christ that these last years have produced. Witness the fact that outside Christendom altogether, in India, for example, men are beginning to look to Jesus of Nazareth for guidance. Witness the new spiritual awakening amongst youth. Witness a score of similar significant facts. One thing is certain: where Jesus is concerned today, the spiritual tide is rising. And it may be that our very generation is going to see the flood coming in across the ramparts of the Church and of the world irresistibly. The fulness of the time is nigh.

So the Redeemer came. Somewhere in the mind and heart

of God from the very foundation of the earth the Christ had been waiting, hidden in the counsels of eternity until the great bell of the ages should strike; and when at last everything in the world and in the souls of men was ready and prepared, He came, the Word of God made flesh, not a moment early and not a moment late, but exactly on the stroke of the hour. It was the Day of the Lord.

It is still the Day of the Lord, whenever another soul enthrones Him. 'Even so, come, Lord Jesus.'

3: CHILDHOOD AND YOUTH

Mon.	Luke i, 26-35	The Angel Messenger
Tues.	Luke i, 46-56	The Song of Mary
Wed.	Luke ii, 8-19	The Fields of Bethlehem
Thur.	Matt. ii, 1-12	The Wise Men from the East
Fri.	Luke ii, 25-40	Age Welcomes Youth
Sat.	Luke ii, 41-52	His Father's Business
Sun.	Luke xi, 5-8; xv, 8-10	
		Memories of a Boyhood Home

Hymnary 47: 'It came upon the midnight clear'
          ,,   65: 'Angels from the realms of glory'

1. The World's Welcome to its Redeemer

It was the fulness of the time. And yet on the day when
Christ entered it, the world looked inhospitable enough.
'There was no room for Him in the inn' (Luke ii, 7). The
innkeeper's refusal to the weary travellers that night was a
foretaste of what was coming. Why did he refuse? He refused partly, no doubt, because he was too busy. The census
of Caesar Augustus was a good thing in its way, he told
himself, for it filled his house with guests and his pockets
with money; but being an innkeeper in census time was no
sinecure, and from early morning till far into the night the
jostling crowds had kept him busy, and certainly he had no
time to waste listening to two belated travellers with a
strange story of distress. He refused, also, because to have
welcomed Joseph and Mary would have meant turning two
of his other guests out, and not under any circumstances, he
told himself, could he do that. Probably he refused, also,
because he saw that the man and woman standing outside in
the cold night were poor and shabby. If Joseph and Mary
had been able to hold up a purse of gold, would there still
have been no room? We wonder. At any rate, it is worth

noticing that the same motives still operate to close the door on Christ. Men are too busy; or they know that if Christ came in, certain other things would have to go; or they set their hearts on something different from One who was poor and lowly and despised and rejected, whose symbol was a Cross. 'He came unto His own, and His own received Him not' (John i, 11).

Yet even so, Christ was not quite unwelcomed. Four deeply significant welcomes the Evangelists record.

(1) *The Evangelists record the welcome of His mother.* Scripture is continually exalting motherhood. In the Decalogue (Exod. xx, 12); in the description of the ideal mother in Proverbs, whose children 'arise up and call her blessed' (Prov. xxxi, 28); in the sublime passage where God Himself takes a mother's love as the nearest thing to His own (Isa. lxvi, 13); and in the noble line of mothers that the portrait-gallery of the Old and New Testaments presents, Hannah, and Ruth and the lady of Shunem, and Elizabeth, and Salome, and Eunice, and many more—motherhood is acclaimed and exalted. But in lonely, unapproached honour stands Mary, the mother of Jesus. From these pages there shines out *her devoutness*. Out of all the women in the world, God chose her to make the home in which the world's Redeemer should be reared. It was at Mary's knee that Jesus lisped His first childhood prayers. There shines out also *her loneliness*. She was lonely in the sublime destiny for which God appointed her, lonely in the deep thoughts she kept and pondered in her heart (Luke ii, 19), lonely on the morning when Jesus left His boyhood home and turned His face to the world, loneliest of all on the the day when 'there stood by the cross of Jesus His mother' (John xix, 25). There shines out also *her glad self-sacrifice*. 'Be it unto me according to Thy word,' she said to God (Luke i, 38); and even when the sword of which Simeon spoke was piercing her (Luke ii, 35), her spirit could still exult in the beauty and strength and holiness of the Son whom God had given her.

(2) *The Evangelists record the welcome of the shepherds.* The story of their presence at the cradle was peculiarly appro-

priate. In ancient Israel, the figure of the shepherd was always closely connected with God, as in that greatest of Israelite songs 'The Lord is my shepherd' (Ps. xxiii). Moreover, the Son of God was to be a shepherd Himself, the Good Shepherd, giving His life for the sheep (John x, 11). And is there not a world of meaning in the fact that it was very ordinary people, busy about very ordinary tasks, whose eyes first saw 'the glory of the coming of the Lord'? It means, first, that the place of duty, however humble, is the place of vision. And it means, second, that it is the men who have kept to the deep, simple pieties of life, and have not lost the child-heart, to whom the gates of the Kingdom most readily open.

Other illustrations of this could be given. To Simon Peter, the vision came out in a boat on the lake in the dawn (Luke v, 8). To Brother Lawrence, it came as he trudged a country road one day, and saw a bare, wintry tree putting forth the first buds of spring. To Joan of Arc, it came in the village church of her girlhood. To Francis Thompson, it came in the roar of London's streets: Jacob's ladder—so he said— was 'pitched betwixt Heaven and Charing Cross'.

(3) *The Evangelists record the welcome of the Wise Men.* Tradition has it that one of these Magi was an African, while the others were Asiatics from Mesopotamia. Their presence at Bethlehem symbolized three things. It symbolized the Gospel's *challenge to adventure*. They had left their far homes for Christ, going out, like Abraham, 'not knowing whither they went'. It symbolized the Gospel's *challenge to thought*. The Magi were the trained investigators, the scientific men of their day, the thinkers. It symbolized the Gospel's *challenge to all the nations of the earth*. Out of the dim East, out of darkest Africa they came (as indeed Israel's singers of old had prophesied, e.g. 'The daughter of Tyre shall be there with a gift,' Ps. xlv, 12; 'Ethiopia shall stretch out her hands unto God,' Ps. lxviii, 31) to lay their national tributes at Jesus' feet.

Thus the Magi represent a threefold challenge of Christianity today. Christ calls for adventurers, especially amongst

B

the Church's youth. Christ calls for thinkers, men who will undertake that most urgent task in our generation, the baptizing of the new knowledge into His name. Christ calls for the tribute of the nations, the wealth of character and loyalty and spiritual understanding that an Aggrey, a Schweitzer, a Kagawa can bring into His Kingdom.*

(4) *The Evangelists record the welcome of Simeon and Anna.* It was the Simeons of that day, 'just and devout, waiting for the consolation of Israel' (Luke ii, 25), who had really saved religion for their land. Not that Palestine was irreligious. It was, indeed, almost too religious. There were the Pharisees. The Pharisees had *externalized* religion, had made it a matter of outward observance, not of the heart. There were the Scribes. The Scribes had *professionalized* religion: they were dry ecclesiastics, not saints with the fire of God in them. There were the Sadducees. The Sadducees had *secularized* religion; they were sceptical and worldly. There were the Zealots. The Zealots had *nationalized* religion, making it a mere adjunct and slave to their one consuming ambition, 'Down with Rome and up with Jewry!' But it was not any official party that had kept the soul of Israel alive. The real saviours of Israel were humble, obscure, devout people, who could not have argued with a scribe or a Sadducee for five minutes, and certainly would not have tried; who could have been made to look foolish by any clever Rabbi, and could not have held a candle to any fiery, loud-voiced, sabre-rattling Zealot; and yet, when it came to the really deep things of life—things like prayer, and the purity of heart that sees God—were a thousand miles beyond all these others. It was Simeon and his like who were the leaven of the land. It was obscure, godly homes like his that were the backbone of Israel.

When Mary brought her Child to the Temple, Simeon took Him up in his arms and blessed Him. Others never turned their heads to look as the peasant-woman and her

---

* Students should be encouraged to read such books as Edwin W. Smith's *Aggrey of Africa*, William Axling's *Kagawa* and Basil Matthews' *The Clash of World Forces*.

Infant passed: but Simeon knew. There is a moral and spiritual qualification for recognizing Jesus and for seeing God, and Simeon had it. Notice, too, that Simeon with the Child Jesus in his arms is a picture of the old welcoming the new. If at his time of life he had been content to dwell mainly or altogether in the past, we could have understood it. But no—his mind was open, and eagerly receptive, and sure that God's best was still to come. So he took the Child—symbol of the new age—and embraced Him in his arms. And then, like a weary toiler hearing the curfew ringing through the gloaming, or like a sentry glad to be relieved at daybreak, he spoke his *Nunc Dimittis*—'Lord, now lettest Thou Thy servant depart in peace, for mine eyes have seen Thy salvation' (Luke ii, 29 f).

So God was incarnate. So through the coming of a little Child the divine work of mending a broken world was begun 'And the Child grew, and waxed strong in spirit, filled with wisdom; and the grace of God was upon Him' (Luke ii, 40).

2. *His Father's Business*

An almost impenetrable veil hangs over the thirty years during which the world's Redeemer was preparing for His work. Legends in plenty about the childhood years of Jesus are recorded by the Apocryphal writers, but these need not concern us. One incident alone shines out like a star in the darkness of the unrecorded years. When He reached the age of twelve Jesus, like other Jewish boys, became a 'Son of the Law', and could attend the religious festivals (Luke ii, 42 ff). (This corresponds roughly to what happens when a boy in Scotland 'joins the Church', and is admitted by profession of faith to full communion.) What His feelings must have been on His first sight of the Holy City and its Temple we can only guess. In the Temple He was found when the festival was over. 'How is it that ye sought Me?' He asked. 'Wist ye not that I must be about My Father's business?' (Luke ii, 49). These are the first words from Jesus' lips that any Evangelist records. And they sum up His whole life. Everything in the story, right on to the Crucifixion, illustrates and proves them. But Joseph and Mary at the time could not understand. Here we have the first hint of that loneliness that was to become so heavy a part of the cross that God's Christ carried (cf. Luke iv, 23 f; John vi, 66; vii, 5).

The Revised Version has made a noteworthy alteration in the translation of this verse. 'Wist ye not that I must be *in My Father's House*?' The Greek text allows either rendering. Whichever we adopt, the one great fact that emerges is Jesus' amazing awareness of God as Father. Amazing, yes; yet in some degree every young life, specially during its adolescent years, may come awake to that same great discovery. Adolescence is God's best chance with the soul.

After this first visit to Jerusalem, the veil falls again and hides another eighteen years. How glad we should have been if the hand of one of the Evangelists had drawn back the veil a little! That more could have been revealed there seems no reason to doubt. Contemporaries of Jesus' boyhood and young manhood in Nazareth could have supplied additional material. Moreover, it is possible that amongst the sources on which St. Luke drew for the compilation of his Gospel was Mary herself; if so, the Evangelist's knowledge of the silent years must have been considerable. But none of our records has chosen to let us into the secret. Perhaps it is better so. The hand that has drawn the veil is the hand of reverence. The silent years of the Redeemer's preparation are holy ground.

3. *Boyhood Influences*

Certain factors, however, which entered into Jesus' preparation for His life-work can be clearly enough discerned. Here we shall mention external factors only: underneath them all lay His deep, constant, secret life of communion with God His Father.

(1) To begin with, there was *Nature*. The Gospels themselves, steeped in Nature-love, are evidence of that. Behind these pictures that have become the possession of Christendom and the spiritual teachers of the world—the lilies decked in glory (Matt. vi, 28 f), the golden miracle of harvest (John

iv, 35), the mystery of unfolding buds (Mark iv, 28), the nesting of the birds (Matt. viii, 20), the folding of the sheep (Luke xv, 4 f), and many another—there lie the observation and the zest of One who was a greater Nature-lover than any poet. Jesus was a country-bred Boy, and on almost every page of the Gospels there is something reminiscent of the youthful Nazareth years when the sights and sounds of Nature 'haunted Him like a passion'.

It is interesting to contrast St. Paul in this respect. Paul was city-bred, and his illustrations, unlike those of Jesus, are drawn almost entirely from crowded places. Builders at work in the streets (1 Cor. iii, 10 ff), the sights and sounds of the military barracks (Eph. vi, 13 ff), the thronged arena of the Greek games (1 Cor. ix, 24 ff)—these, rather than country scenes, are Paul's chosen metaphors. But the Gospel pages are scented with winds that have blown across hills and valleys and fields of springing corn; and God's care and mercy are over all.

(2) But if Nature was one factor influencing the preparation of the silent years, *Human Nature* was another. Here again the Gospels are our witness. The children playing in the market-place, and sometimes growing sulky in their play (Matt. xi, 16 f); the woman pestering the local magistrate until by sheer doggedness she gains her point (Luke xviii, 1 ff); the country lad going away to see life in the great city and coming back broken and penniless and ashamed (Luke xv, 11 ff); the professional religionist parading his piety before a gaping group of idlers at the corner of the village street (Matt. vi, 5); these and many other pictures reveal the student of human nature. The silent Nazareth years must have been full of that study. 'He knew all men, and required no evidence from anyone about human nature; well did He know what was in human nature' (John ii, 25, Moffatt). But Jesus was much more than a student of His fellow-men. He was a lover of men. Through all the tragedy and comedy of life, through all their human foibles and bignesses of soul, through sin and the pitiful consequences of sin, He loved them as only God could love.

(3) A third factor was *Scripture*. Jesus' Bible was the Old Testament. This was the foundation stone of all Jewish education; and from early childhood Jesus, like all Jewish children, would be brought up in the atmosphere of Genesis and Deuteronomy and the Psalms and Isaiah and Jeremiah. Long hours of His growing manhood must have been given to poring over the sacred page. And He studied it to some purpose. When the Tempter came to Him in the desert, it was with a quotation from the Old Testament that each of the three temptations was rebutted (Matt. iv, 4, 7, 10). In the great prophetic picture of the invasion of human life by the divine Spirit (Isa. lxi, 1 ff) He saw His own work foreshadowed (Luke iv, 18 ff). And how powerfully the thought of the Suffering Servant (Isa. liii) influenced His own conception of the Messianic vocation we can realize again and again throughout the Gospel story. His soul was steeped in the great old Scriptures of His people.

Hebrew, which had ceased to be the spoken tongue, was the mother-tongue of Judaism; and though the Scriptures had been translated into Greek (in the Septuagint), it was in Hebrew that Jesus read and studied them. In the common speech of the day, Hebrew had given place to Aramaic, a derivative of the same Semitic family. But with the coming of Greek, Palestine had become bilingual. No doubt, while able to use Greek at will, Jesus would familiarly think and speak in the Aramaic of the vernacular. Our Gospels, written in Greek, have preserved (possibly because of the emotion of the circumstances in which they were originally spoken) certain Aramaic expressions of our Lord's—'Talitha cumi' (Mark v, 41), 'Ephphatha' (Mark vii, 34), and 'Eloi, Eloi, lama sabachthani' (Mark xv, 34). But His Old Testament quotations make it clear that He had studied His Bible in the original Hebrew.

(4) A fourth factor in the unrecorded preparatory years was *the workshop*. Jesus was Carpenter of Nazareth. It is impossible to exhaust the significance of the fact that for a great part of His life on earth the Son of God toiled with His hands, doing a joiner's work. 'A workshop', said Henry

Drummond, 'is not a place for making engines so much as a place for making men.' A workshop helped to make the soul of Christ. The devoted skill and labour that went into those Nazareth yokes and ploughs and cottage tables were rendered as an offering to God. Even then Jesus was 'about His Father's business'. Hence toil has been hallowed for ever. The distinction between secular and sacred avocations vanishes. Hard work—whether manual labour or the duty of the business man—*is* sacred when it is done as under the eyes of God.

> Very dear the Cross of shame,
> Where He took the sinner's blame. . . .
> But He walked the same high road,
> And He bore the self-same load
> When the Carpenter of Nazareth
> Made common things for God.

There is a legend that over the door of the Carpenter's shop there was the sign—'My yokes are easy' (cf. Matt. xi, 30). Whether the sign was there or not, we can well believe that every yoke made in the shop in Nazareth was light and easy and well-fitting. Made by the same hands, the yoke for the oxen at the plough and the yokes for the disciples of the Kingdom were alike in that.

(5) Finally, there was *the home*. It must never be forgotten that Jesus was brought up in the heart of a big family (Matt. xiii, 55 ff; Mark vi, 3). Joseph seems to have died comparatively early, for his name disappears from the narrative altogether; and no doubt when Jesus grew to manhood it was upon Him, as the eldest brother, that the main responsibility for the support of the home devolved. Sidelights upon the early home-life of the Master may be found in many of the parables. The turning-out of the house to find a coin that has rolled away into a dark corner and disappeared (Luke xv, 8 ff); the measuring of the flour and the leaven for the weekly baking (Matt. xiii, 33); the plight of the householder who, finding his larder empty on the arrival of an untimely guest, knocks up his churlish neighbour at midnight (Luke xi, 5 ff); the lighting of the candles at the gloaming hour

(Matt. v, 15); the healthy appetites of children home from school and play (Matt. vii, 9 f)—these touches and many others are surely reminiscent of Mary's home, a home from which in days when trade was bad poverty could not be very far away. Certainly there was no affluence about it. 'Is not this the carpenter's son?' they said later, and there was no mistaking the sneer (Matt. xiii, 55). But to Jesus it was home, and love was there, and God was there; and by His own devotion to it all those hidden, waiting years, He has hallowed home-life for ever.

Such were the factors that entered into our Lord's preparation for His life-work. Thirty long years passed and no sign was given. There was a broken world to be mended, a lost humanity to be redeemed, and still there was no sign. Then, quite suddenly, God's hour struck; and the Son of Man came forth.

4: THE COMING OF THE CALL

Mon. 1 Sam. iii, 1-10   The Call of God
Tues. Luke i, 59-80   The Birth of the Forerunner
Wed. John i, 15-28   A Voice in the Wilderness
Thur. Matt. iii, 1-12 The Beginning of the Revival
Fri. John i, 29-37   Behold the Lamb of God
Sat. Matt. iii, 13-17   The Baptism of Jesus
Sun. Mark vi, 14-29   The Death of the Baptist

Psalm i: 'That man hath perfect blessedness'
Hymnary 141: 'Immortal Love, for ever full'

1. *A Voice in the Wilderness*

There is always something strangely moving and fascinating in the sight of a young soul launching out into the deep and entering upon its life-work. The day when God calls you to do something—whether that call be to run a business, or to teach a school, or to work in an office, or to preach the Gospel—is one of life's great crucial days. Here we have the story of the most momentous call in history, the call of Jesus to His work of saving the world.

On one point all four Gospels are agreed: Christ's call was in some way connected with John the Baptist's preaching and with the whirlwind revival which that preaching had started. Our first step, then, is to look at this man of the desert and try to probe his secret and his power.

If you had asked any of the people in the crowds that flocked out to the Jordan to hear him what that secret and that power were, they would almost certainly have fixed on three things: this John was a man, he was a man of God, and he was a man with a message.

He was a man. He radiated vitality and virility. Even the way he lived made them feel that. For out there in the desert he had dispensed with all the mere accessories of life, clothed himself in the roughest, simplest clothing as a protest against the overdone purples and soft raiments of so many who called themselves religious, and lived on locusts and wild honey, subsisting on the bare minimum in order to prove that a man's life consisteth not in the abundance of the things which he possesseth (Luke xii, 15). The very way he lived convinced the world that this was a man indeed.

Moreover, they knew him for a man by his attitude to the whole question of popularity. The very last thing John resembled was a 'reed shaken with the wind' (Matt. xi, 7). Human applause and approbation meant simply nothing to him. Smooth, conventional inanities his soul hated. If a thing was true, then out with it—though they should turn and rend him for it. Pericles, the great Greek (so we are told by Plutarch), never spoke without leaving a secret sting in the hearts of his hearers. That was the Baptist's way.

You see it in his attitude to the Pharisees and Sadducees, the great men of the land. 'O generation of vipers, who hath warned you to flee?' (Matt. iii, 7). You see it still better in his attitude to Herod. Herod first patronized him, applauded him, showered marks of favour on him; and Herod, remember, was a king, and it is surely something big for a desert prophet to be taken up and courted by a king. Surely the prophet will be careful in his speech, more apologetic, more ready to turn a blind eye to certain ways and practices. Will he indeed? Herod might be a king, but there was a King above kings; and if the royal law of Heaven were broken, then straight into Herod's presence John would go with flashing eyes and pointing finger and blunt rebuke: 'It is not lawful for thee!' (Matt. xiv, 4). Here was a real man. F. W. H. Myers' splendid lines are true:

> John, than which man a grander or a greater
>   Not till this day has been of woman born,
> John like some iron peak by the Creator
>   Fired with the red glow of the rushing morn.

But he was more than a man, he was a *man of God*. That,

too, drew the crowds flocking out to the desert, that here for the first time in their lives they had come upon a religion utterly and absolutely real, a religion real in every flaming syllable of it, real in every burning word. 'To teach religion', said Thomas Carlyle, 'the first thing needful and the last, and indeed the only thing, is to find a man who *has* religion.' Here was a man who had religion, whose whole life and attitude breathed God!

Now that was something new. These people had been in the habit of taking their religion from the scribes, and with the scribes it was all a mass of learned subtleties and intricate sophistries, a poor, discredited, second-hand affair. But here was this new voice, blowing all that to the winds, and going right to the heart of things, like Amos seven hundred years before—'The lion hath roared, who will not fear? The Lord God hath spoken, who can but prophesy?' (Amos iii, 8). John, like Amos, came with a ringing 'Thus saith the Lord!' That was what won these people, that here at last—surprisingly and overwhelmingly—was religion utterly real. A man of God indeed!

He was a man, and a man of God. He was also *a man with a message*. Indeed, so absorbed was he in the message he had received from God for men that he forgot all about himself; his own personality was lost, swallowed up in the truth he was charged to deliver. For when the priests and Levites were sent out to investigate, and asked him who he was, his answer was—'I am the voice of one crying in the wilderness, Make straight the way of the Lord,' a voice, and nothing more. The man was nothing, the message everything. And what was the message? Nothing gentle or soft or soothing; but this, with a terrible urgency behind it, and a passionate pleading in every note of it—'Repent! Flee from the wrath to come!'

> Also of John a calling and a crying
>> Rang in Bethabara, till strength was spent,
> Cared not for counsel, stayed not for replying,
>> John had one message for the world, 'Repent.'

2. The Revival

Now let us turn from the preacher to his crowd. He did not have to go in search of an audience. They came in spite of themselves. And a motley audience it was. Soldiers were there and publicans, poor folk and saddened sinners, rubbing shoulders with proud, self-satisfied Pharisees and sceptical Sadducees. The very audience proves that it was no manmade thing, this revival, but the power of the everlasting God.

What were the motives that drew them? *Some no doubt came from curiosity.* There were Jerusalem circles where it was the fashion to be able to say you had been out in the desert hearing John; and there were people there, no less than at Athens, who lived for any new thing that was happening. It is worth while remarking that in religion the motive of curiosity still operates. There are people who, if a revival started, would be right in the thick of it, not so much for any definitely spiritual reason as just for the new sensation. But that motive of curiosity is not to be sneered at: many a soul that came to look on (like Zacchaeus) has stayed to pray.

Others again flocked out to John *for political reasons.* For two hundred years the voice of prophecy had been silent in Israel, and now down by the Jordan it had burst out again. What could that mean but this, that a new nationalist movement was on the way, and that the heel of the oppressor was to be shaken from Israel's throat? 'Down with Rome and up with Jewry!' was the cry.

But there was a better motive than either curiosity or nationalism: there were men in that crowd who were there *because they had sins to confess.* These were the men the Baptist wanted. Every day, when his fiery preaching was over, they stayed behind for private talks; and one by one he dealt with them, helping them to make a clean breast of all life's guilty secrets, and carrying them right out into the feeling of release and liberation that making a clean breast to one understanding heart always gives. Then he took them down to the water, and baptized them for the new life. And soon his converts were scattering the glory of it across the land.

3. Jesus and John

By and by the news of the revival reached Galilee. It reached the streets and cottages of Nazareth. It reached a humble workshop where a young Carpenter was toiling at His bench. And Jesus knew that God's hour had struck, and that the sign He had been waiting for was come. That same day He rose and went.

But what was Jesus' attitude to John, and to John's revival, to be? Clearly there were three possible attitudes.

(1) For one thing, Jesus might easily have stood aloof. He might have told Himself that this was a baptism of confession and repentance, and He had nothing to confess or to repent. For these others, it was all very well, a God-sent blessing for them in their sins—but it could not be for Him.

(2) Again, He might have challenged and criticized it. John's gospel was so obviously imperfect, just a half-gospel indeed: ought Christ to countenance it? There were two defects in it which Christ saw.

On the one hand, it was so terribly negative. John's followers, as Jesus Himself said at a later day, were like children in the market-place playing at funerals, whereas Mine want to dance! The very fact that John was a desert man, an ascetic, told against him, and proved that he had somehow missed the rapturous, radiant, happy-hearted view of God for which Christ stood. 'I'll think more of your prayers', wrote Robert Louis Stevenson to his father, 'when I see more of your praises!' That was where John came short, with his 'Thou shalt not' religion.

Moreover, here, saw Jesus, was a religion built on fear. 'Flee from the wrath to come.' Is fear a fit weapon for driving men into salvation? Here was John preaching a flaming God, and here was Christ with His heart throbbing with the news of a Father God: ought Christ to countenance John? He might have opposed him. Andrew Bonar and Robert Murray M'Cheyne were walking together one day. 'M'Cheyne asked me', says Bonar, 'what my last Sabbath's subject had been. It had been: "The wicked shall be turned into hell." On hearing this awful text, he asked: "Were you able to preach it with tenderness?" ' There was too little tenderness about the Baptist's preaching, too much flame and denunciation: and Jesus, with His tender, loving heart, might have refused to identify Himself with it in any way.

(3) But there was a third possible attitude, and it was this Jesus took. He did not oppose, nor did He stand aloof; but in the terrific humility of God's only Son He went to John. 'Sir, I would fain be baptized of thee!'

Probably it was late at evening it happened, when the day's crowds had dispersed, and the Baptist, weary and spent, was left alone in prayer. Through the gloaming came a solitary figure, bronzed and young and clean and godlike. And when the Baptist, rising from his knees, met Him, and looked into His face, and saw shining out from the eyes of Him a light he had never seen before, very God of very God, and when he heard that request, 'I would be baptized of thee,' suddenly the incongruity of it overwhelmed him. 'I have need to be baptized of Thee, and comest Thou to me?' But the quiet voice answered—'Suffer it to be so now: for thus it becometh us to fulfil all righteousness.' And with that, they went down into the water together and there happened the event which the very angels might desire to look into—a man baptizing his Lord.

4. *The Inner Meaning of the Baptism of Jesus*

How are we to interpret this mystery—the sinless Jesus undergoing a baptism meant for sinners?

Sometimes the view has been expressed that as this was a baptism of repentance, Jesus must have felt that He Himself, like all His brothers of the earth, had something to repent of. Would He have sought a baptism for the remission of sins, if He had not been conscious of sin? This we can safely reject without more ado.

It seems likely that Jesus was moved to act as He did partly, at least, because *He felt a real debt to John*. Here was a nation-wide movement of revival. Spiritual issues, which for long years had been suffering from neglect, had suddenly leapt into the foreground. Young people and old had begun to take religion seriously. Men were worrying about their sins. They were hungry for spiritual guidance. They were crying for the light of God. Now obviously all this gave Jesus an enormously hopeful atmosphere in which to begin His work. Defective as the message of the Baptist's mission was at certain points, it was nevertheless a wonderful preparation for the Gospel. John was a true forerunner. And we may well believe that when Jesus offered Himself for baptism, He did it partly, at least, from a sense of the debt He owed to His great predecessor, and from a recognition that this revival which had been sweeping the land was a real movement of the Spirit of God.

But there was another motive which must be taken into account. Jesus went down into the Jordan *to take His stand by the side of sinners.* When you see the sinless Christ going to the sinners' baptism, you are seeing love going to a great redeeming act of self-identification. It was a prophecy of what the coming years were to bring, when the Lord of glory was to earn the name 'Friend of publicans and sinners', to go where need called, reckless of His reputation, to sit often at outcasts' tables, and to die at last between two thieves. 'He was numbered with the transgressors' (Isa. liii, 12). True, but He numbered Himself with them first of all. At the Jordan, Jesus took His stand by the side of sinners, making their shame His shame, their trouble His trouble, their penitence His penitence, their burden His burden. It was the beginning of the work that was crowned at Calvary, when He carried the burden away for ever.

Hence the baptism of Jesus points the fact that the only love which can ever possess redeeming power is a love that goes all the way and identifies itself with others. So Moses, in the day of his people's sin, stood and cried—'Blot *me,* I pray Thee, out of Thy book of life which Thou hast written' (Exod. xxxii, 32). So Paul, lamenting the blindness of his nation, exclaimed—'I could wish that myself were accursed from Christ for my brethren, my kinsmen according to the flesh' (Rom. ix, 3). George Fox prayed 'to be baptized' (note the word) 'into a sense of all conditions, that I might know the needs and feel the sorrows of all.' Father Damien's self-identification meant literal leprosy. 'Whenever I preach to my people', he said, 'I do not say, "my brethren", as you do, but "we lepers". People pity me and think me unfortunate, but I think myself the happiest of missionaries.' 'Do you think that I care for my soul if my boy be gone to the fire?' cries the mother in Tennyson's *Rizpah*. It is that same self-identifying love of which Jesus' baptism speaks.

In the great moment of Jesus' baptism, says the narrative, two things came to Him—a Voice and a Vision. The Voice spoke to Him out of heaven, and in the Vision of the dove the Holy Spirit descended. The Voice was the call for which through the 'silent years' at Nazareth He had been waiting, the call to His life-work; the Spirit was the equipment for obeying the call and for carrying out the work. 'Thou art My beloved Son, in whom I am well pleased'—that swept the last hesitation from Jesus' soul, and the Messianic vocation was accepted. And with the Vision came the endowment for Messiahship: the sense of power flooded His soul. The Spirit of God, which had been brooding over creation from the first (Gen. i, 2), haunting the dreams of saints (Ps. cxxxix, 7), and breaking out intermittently in the words of prophets (Isa. lxi, 1), was now focused and concentrated to one burning point in Jesus' soul; and He came up from the water, the Called of the Father, the Power of God unto salvation.

5: THE DESERT

1. *The Background of the Story*

One or two preliminary questions meet us on the threshold of this story.

How did the story come to be in the Gospels at all? The Master's fight with Satan happened out in a desert, far from the beaten track and the eyes of men. During those forty days and nights Jesus was utterly alone, with not another soul anywhere near Him, not a disciple or a friend or anyone to see what happened and tell the story afterwards. Yet the Evangelists are able to give a vivid and detailed account. How has that come about? Clearly there is only one explanation: the story came direct from the lips of Christ Himself.

Why did Jesus tell it? That chapter of His life was closed: why did He go back to it and bring it to light? Certainly not to gratify anyone's curiosity. Certainly not to provide additional biographical materials for posterity or to supply an extra chapter in our Gospels. Probably there were two reasons. First, Jesus shared this experience with His disciples in order to help them through their own tempted hours. It does help greatly, as everyone who has ever been tempted knows, to hear of some other's fight and victory. And if that other should be Christ—how mightily it helps! But second, Jesus told this story because the titanic struggle of the desert days and nights had marked His soul for ever, and He could never forget. He could see and feel it after months as plainly as if it had happened only yesterday—the wild, desolate loneliness, the rocks and crags with the pitiless sun beating down on them by day and the biting night wind moaning across them in the dark, the prowling beasts, the famishing hunger, the demon voices whispering to His heart, the grace of God and the angels that had brought Him through. Jesus told His disciples of it because He could not help it. It would not hide.

What does this imply about the Temptation? It means that Christ's temptation was real, literally, desperately real. Now that needs to be said emphatically; for many people are quite sure that it was not and cannot have been real, at least not as our own familiar, dogged temptations are. That idea springs from a praiseworthy motive of doing honour to Jesus. 'Surely', it is said, 'if Jesus were the Son of God, He must always have done the right thing without any struggle at all. The very possibility of inward conflict is excluded.' But is it? It may be glorifying Jesus to say He won His victory always without effort. But surely it is glorifying Him far more to say He marched to it through an agony of sweat and blood. And indeed the whole Gospel and our own hopes of salvation are bound up with a Christ who was 'tempted in all points'—not just here and there, but in all points—'like as we are' (Heb. iv, 15). The dramatic story of it is told in a pictorial, symbolical way; but what we have to remember is that the experience itself was wholly inward. As we see Jesus then, we see Him not with any great, gaunt, black-winged Satan beside Him (as children's picture-books sometimes present the scene), not that at all: we see Jesus quite alone, sitting on a spur of rock, with His head bowed and His hands clenched, and then falling down on His knees, and then on His face, with a cry breaking from Him that sounds like—'Oh God, if it be possible, let this cup pass';

and then we turn our eyes away, for it is an awful thing to see the Son of God like that. The writer to the Hebrews settled it once for all when he penned the brief, terrific words —'He hath suffered, being tempted' (ii, 18).

When did this desert experience come? It came immediately after the Baptism. That is quite vital to an understanding of it. Indeed, it may be said that it was what happened at the Baptism that caused the Temptation. For there, down in the water of the Jordan, with the heavens opening above Him and the voice of God speaking right home to His heart, Jesus had suddenly grown conscious of His Messianic power. He had come up out of the water with His whole being throbbing with that exultant discovery. And it was then the Tempter struck. This new, magnificent power—how was it to be used? All three temptations turn on that.

2. *The First Temptation: the Spiritual versus the Material*

Alone in the wilderness, after days and nights of prayer and meditation and fasting, Jesus was starving. And there was no help at hand, unless—'Make the stones bread!' said a sudden voice within.

Now that temptation attacked Jesus along three lines. *It attacked Him along the line of His new-found power.* Would this not be a splendid chance to test that power, to see if it really worked, to prove whether it was something more than an imagination and a dream? 'Son of God'—but *was* He Son of God? 'Try it!' said Satan. 'Put it to the proof!'

It attacked Him along the line of His vocation. God was needing Jesus for His work. God, He knew, had a tremendous mission waiting Him down the future years, and if He died out there in the desert with all that unfulfilled—what then? Would He not be defeating God? Would He not be robbing the world of its Messiah, and men of their salvation, and God of His Kingdom? Was it not His duty to save Himself? 'Make the stones bread,' said Satan.

It attacked Him along the line of His love for men. For surely it was not His own hunger alone that was in Jesus' thoughts in these desert days. There was the hunger of the great multitudes of the world's poor, the desperate, appalling need of the shepherdless hosts of Palestine and beyond who had barely enough to keep body and soul together. If He were the Son of God ought He not, for their sakes, to make the stones bread? The question here was not one of an occasional gift of food to the hungry, such as the Evangelists subsequently record: it was a question of the regular method to be adopted for His whole public career. Ought He not to use His power to satisfy men's bodily needs, and so gain a short-cut to their affections? Then, after that, He would be able to do anything, absolutely anything, with them, to sweep whole grateful multitudes of them straight into the Kingdom of God! First the earthly Paradise, then the heavenly Paradise—was that not the right order? 'In the name of your compassion for men', said the Tempter, 'make the stones bread.'

It was subtle, Satanically subtle. But Jesus refused. Why? We can discern two reasons.

Suppose He had consented. Suppose that, having eaten, and feeling now like a giant refreshed, He had turned His back on the desert and made for the crowded streets again, travelling in the greatness of His strength. What then? *Then Christ the Brother and Comrade would have been lost to us for ever.* For no longer would He have been standing shoulder to shoulder with us in our human pains and privations and troubles. Never again could we have sung:

> Our fellow-suff'rer yet retains
> A fellow-feeling of our pains;
> And still remembers in the skies
> His tears, His agonies, and cries.

It was in the name of His brotherhood with men that Jesus rejected the Tempter and hurled his suggestion back with scorn.

But again Jesus refused, *because He had come into the world to win men, not to bribe them.* That does not imply for a moment that Jesus was indifferent to men's material needs and social conditions. Indeed, He cared far more about these things than any reformer or politician or philanthropist who has ever lived. Sometimes His followers have forgotten that. But we have been rediscovering it. We know now that until the cry for bread—and that includes the cry for a decent home and a clean environment and a Christianized social order—is answered, there can be no rest for Christ, and no rest for the Church, and no rest for any of us who call Him Lord. But our point just now is that when, in spite of all that, in spite of His passionate longing to see the earth a garden of God, Jesus refused the short-cut of making the stones bread, it was because He was in the world to win men, not to bribe them. He knew there was a hunger in the human heart deeper and stronger and more insistent than the hunger for bread and material things. And it was that deeper hunger, that nameless longing of the soul which can be satisfied, not with bread, nor riches, nor any material comforts whatever, but only with the broken body of God—it was that Christ came to appease. The Bread He gave was Himself.

3. *The Second Temptation: the Lure of the Spectacular*

It is worth emphasizing the fact that there *was* a second temptation. It might have been thought that Jesus, having gained His victory once, had gained it for ever. But there, too, He shared our human experience: and we can remember for our comfort, when old beaten foes come back with stubborn doggedness, that Christ was tempted not once nor twice, but many times, and not only in the desert, but throughout His life.

There was a day, for example, months afterwards, when His best friend tried to save Him from Himself, and begged Him for pity's sake to turn aside before it was too late and avoid the Cross (Matt. xvi, 22 f). 'Be it far from Thee, Lord,' said Peter, 'this shall not be unto Thee.' Whereupon, says the Evangelist, Jesus suddenly turned round on Peter with the cry, 'Get thee behind Me, Satan.' There is a note of tension in that which can only mean that Jesus was being tempted then almost more than He could bear. Even on Calvary the Tempter came again, and made a last desperate bid: 'If Thou be the Son of God, come down from the cross' (Matt. xxvii, 40). So Jesus, like ourselves, had to fight again and again. 'The devil departed from Him', says Luke significantly, *'for a season'* (iv, 13).

To understand the second temptation, remember that Jesus in the desert days and nights was thinking out His life-work and the methods He would follow. He knew that God had sent Him to save the world. But how best to do it? Suppose He confined Himself to preaching. Would they listen? Would they respond? It seemed doubtful, to say the least of it. It was then the Tempter struck in, suggesting another way, a far surer way. Why confine Himself to the simple Gospel? Why not do something startling, dramatic, spectacular? That would bring the world to His feet. So the wild idea of the leap from the Temple pinnacle broke upon His mind.

But Jesus rejected it. Why?

'Thou shalt not tempt [make wilful proof of] the Lord thy God' (Matt. iv, 7). That was one reason for His refusal. The spectacular leap would not have been an act of trust in God at all: it would have been flinging a challenge in God's face and forcing God's hand. Jesus would not have anything to do with that. That, to Jesus, was sin.

Again, suppose He had done it—*would it really have effected its purpose?* Would it have saved a single soul? It would, no doubt, have called out an immediate burst of admiration and applause. It would certainly not have bound them to Him for life. Men may acclaim something that stirs their imagination: but they can be saved only by something that touches the heart.

Moreover, it was always against the grain with Jesus *to appeal to the lower side of men's nature and the sensationalist spirit.* Men might want Him to blaze His message across the skies, to stop the stars in their courses, to call down fire from heaven, to change the face of nature; but no one knew better than Christ that that spirit had absolutely nothing to do with religion at all. That was not the Messiah spirit, but the Herod spirit. (See Luke xxiii, 8.)

Finally, *Jesus would never violate the freedom of men's wills.*
And that, too, the leap from the pinnacle would have involved. It would have been overriding their calmer judgement. It would have been forcing a confession of faith. That
was one thing that Jesus definitely would not do. If He
could not win men into salvation by sheer goodness and love,
He was not going to force them into it by miracles and magic.
'Behold, I stand at the door, and knock. *If any man open the
door*, I will come in.'

4. *The Third Temptation: the Way of Compromise*

Here, again, it is important to remember that it was the
Master's life-work that was the issue. The passion of His
life was to win the wide earth for God, to bind all the kingdoms of the world and the glory of them to God's great
throne for ever. What the Tempter now suggested was that
the easiest, quickest, surest way to do it would be to lower
His demands from men, to haul down the flag of the faith
ever so little, to come to terms with the world-powers. One
moment kneeling at my feet, said Satan, and your dream will
be true!

'Get thee hence!' Jesus rejected the compromise. Why?
Because He knew it would be the death of religion to ask
anything less than the whole.

Very nobly the early Church followed its Master there. It
is an extraordinarily significant fact that of all the new religions that came pouring in to Rome out of the East in the
early centuries the religion of Jesus was the only one to
arouse real persecution. When the religions of Osiris, Cybele,
and other gods and goddesses came, Rome welcomed them
all with open arms. But when the lonely God from Palestine
came, and the Nazarene's name was first heard on the imperial streets, Rome girded herself to fight Him to the death.
Why? It was because Osiris and the rest were content to live
together and share the honours: but the young God with
the nailprints in His hands would not live together or share
the honours with any. From the day of Jesus' decision in the
desert, the demand of His religion was all or nothing.

And from the day of that decision, Calvary was inevitable: a demand like that will always mean a Cross. Hence the fury with which Rome persecuted His followers, hunted them down to the catacombs, burned them in the arena, threw them to the lions, flung them outside the camp to bear Christ's reproach. It was because it was obedient to that decision in the desert that the Church, like its Lord, was crucified, dead, and buried; and it was because it was obedient to the decision that the Church, again like its Lord, broke the grave and went out conquering and to conquer. For the road which Jesus faced when He refused to compromise is the hard road, the long road, the sacrificial road; but it is the royal road to the Kingdom.

5. *Two Practical Conclusions*

The study of the Temptation narrative illuminates two important points.

On the one hand, it proves that *temptation is not necessarily sin.* Men like Peter and John might easily have been brought by the persistence of their personal temptations almost to despair. They had seen the vision splendid and had left all to follow it, and yet temptations sprang upon them distressingly—until they may well have questioned the reality of their own discipleship and thought themselves tainted with ineradicable sin. But from the moment when Jesus narrated this story to them, the sting was taken out of that perplexity. For the thought of Jesus, the fairest, cleanest, noblest soul in all the earth, yet carrying the sweat of almost unbearable temptation upon His brow, settled it once for all (and it ought to settle it for troubled, sensitive souls today): temptation is not sin.

On the other hand, the narrative illuminates the great saying of a later disciple—'*In that He Himself hath suffered being tempted, He is able to succour them that are tempted*' (Heb. ii, 18). Peter and John and the rest verified that anew every day they lived with Him. For as time went on, they found that they could conquer the love of the world in themselves, and indeed every low love, not by crushing it down by sheer force of will, but by having a better love to set against it, the love of Jesus, who had gone the same hard road Himself. Contact with His radiant, dynamic personality achieved the impossible. God's own victorious power was coming across into their weak lives, not through any moral code, impersonal and cold and uninspiring, but through this splendid, magnificent, adorable Lover of their souls; not by any strained and difficult obedience, but by 'Christ in them the hope of glory'. 'He is able,' they said. That is the heart and centre of Christianity—yesterday, today, and for ever.

6: THE GOSPEL OF THE KINGDOM

Mon. Micah iv, 1-8   The Jewish Expectation
Tues. Luke x, 17-24; xvii, 20-21
                         The Kingdom already Present
Wed. Matt. xiii, 44-46 The Search for the Kingdom
Thur. John iii, 1-8
                         The Entrance Gate of the Kingdom
Fri. Matt. xiii, 24-33 The Growth of the Kingdom
Sat. Matt. xxv, 1-13
                         The Consummation of the Kingdom
Sun. Matt. v, 1-12   The Kingdom Character

Hymnary 153: 'Thy Kingdom come'
     „   388: 'Jesus shall reign'

1. *The Watchword*

Every new idea that has ever burst upon the world has had a watchword. Always there has been some word or phrase in which the very genius of the thing has been concentrated and focused, some word or phrase to blazon on its banners when it went marching out into the world. Islam had a watchword: 'God is God, and Mohammed is His prophet.' The French Revolution had a watchword: 'Liberty, Equality, Fraternity'. The democratic idea had a watchword: 'Government of the people, by the people, for the people'. The Student Volunteer Missionary Union had a watchword: 'The Evangelization of the World in this Generation'. Every new idea that has stirred the hearts of men has created its own watchword, something to wave like a flag, to rally the ranks and win recruits. Now the greatest idea that has ever been born upon the earth is the Christian idea. And Christianity came with a watchword, magnificent and mighty and imperial; and the watchword was: 'The Kingdom of God'.

46

Every great leader who has ever arisen among the sons of men has been possessed by one master-thought. Always there has been some one thought that has gripped the man like a passion, one truth that has burned in his sky like a Greenland sun, never setting night or day. Socrates had a master-thought: the immortality of the soul. Buddha had a master-thought: the renunciation of life. Napoleon had a master-thought: the domination of Europe. Luther had a master-thought: the freedom of the individual. Every great leader who has towered up above the sons of men has had some one thought that held and haunted and dominated him, one thought that drove a passage for him through this close-grained earth and lifted him high. Now the greatest Leader who has ever led the hosts of humanity is Jesus Christ. And Jesus, like all these others, came with *His* master-thought, glorious and thrilling, world-shaking and world-transforming, and Christ's master-thought was 'the Kingdom of God'.

In the Gospels themselves the name 'kingdom of God' occurs over a hundred times. The first sermon of Jesus' earthly ministry, says Mark, had this for its subject—'The time is fulfilled, and the kingdom of God is at hand' (Mark i, 15). The last sermon of His earthly ministry had the same great theme, for when Jesus came back to His own for a time after Calvary, says the Book of Acts, He spoke to them 'of the things pertaining to the kingdom of God' (Acts i, 3). And if the beginning and the end of Christ's ministry struck that one note, it was also kept sounding all the way through. Think of the parables. How many of them begin—'The kingdom of God is like . . .'! Think of Christ's commission to His followers. 'Into whatsoever city ye enter, say unto them, The kingdom of God is come nigh unto you' (Luke x, 8 f). Here we have the watchword of the evangel. But what does it mean? What did Jesus mean by it? The trouble is that we are apt to read our own ideas into it. We are apt to take out of it our own thoughts about religion. What we have to do is to ask, not what does the name 'kingdom of God' mean as popularly used today, not what do we think it ought to mean, but what did Jesus mean by it? That, and only that, is our concern now.

2. The Kingdom in Judaism

First it will be well to get this clear, that while the thought was original with Jesus, the name itself was not. To Jewish ears, 'kingdom of God' had a familiar sound, and in Jewish writings it had a prominent place. To take only one instance out of many, there is the great cry that breaks out of the Book of Daniel (vii, 14): 'His dominion is an everlasting dominion, and His kingdom that which shall not be destroyed.' Now to understand Jesus' position, it is important to observe that in the generation immediately before Jesus two things had happened to this Jewish thought of the kingdom. On the one hand, it had suddenly become redoubled in intensity. That was the direct result of the foreign domination and oppression; for with Rome's heel on Israel's throat, the only hope was that God would strike in and make His kingdom come. On the other hand, it had been almost completely secularized. Material splendours, political aggrandizement, secular benefits—these were the things on which the popular mind was set, and all spiritual expectations were swamped. Even the men Jesus chose for His disciples found it hard to break away from the prevailing secularism; and when James and John demanded the best places in the kingdom (Matt. xx, 20), or when after the Resurrection the disciples asked, 'Lord, wilt Thou at this time restore again the kingdom to Israel?' (Acts i, 6), it showed how deeply-rooted the earthly, political, unspiritual ideas of the kingdom were. In short, the 'kingdom of God' had come to be the slogan of Jewish nationalism.

Subsequent history shows how strong and unquenchable the nationalist spirit can be. We think of a Mazzini in Italy, a Sun Yat-sen in China, a Gandhi in India, each of them fostering the nationalist spirit and fanning it to a blaze. Certainly that spirit has a real part to play in the evolution of the race. But equally certainly God never meant it to be an end in itself. Over and above the sentiment of nationality,

God looks to His people to develop a fellowship that will be supranational, non-exclusive, world-embracing.

Never in the whole course of history has the nationalist spirit been stronger than in the Judaism of Jesus' day. 'How is it', a woman once said to Jesus, 'that Thou, being a Jew, askest drink of me, which am a woman of Samaria?' And the Evangelist adds the explanatory note—'The Jews have no dealings with the Samaritans' (John iv, 9). That was what Jewish nationalism had become. It had entrenched itself even in the Temple, the last place surely where it ought to have intruded. There, between the outer court of the Gentiles and the inner court of the Jews, stood a barrier with this written on it—'Let no foreigner enter within. Whosoever is taken so doing will himself be the cause that death overtakes him.' And when the Jewish mind dreamed of its Messiah, it was as a kind of super Judas Maccabaeus that it envisaged him, driving his way with drawn sword to the throne of an earthly kingdom. Indeed, in the name 'kingdom of God', nearly all the emphasis was being thrown upon 'kingdom', and very little of it upon 'God'. Only the name was there, awaiting the day when it would be re-born and baptized into Christ.

That day arrived. Jesus found this name waiting. He took it, transformed it beyond all recognition, and made it central in His message. Jesus put so much into it, and brought out so many different aspects of it, that it is difficult to reduce His meaning to any single formula or definition. But clearly there were two main lines along which all His thoughts of the kingdom ran. On the one hand, He thought of it as the rule of God in the heart. On the other hand, He thought of it as the rule of God in the world. Let us take these two aspects separately.

3. *The Kingdom as the Rule of God in the Heart*

When Jesus proclaimed this and made it a foundation stone of His Gospel, He was really drawing three vital distinctions, every one of which laid the axe to the root of prevailing, popular conceptions. If the kingdom was the rule of God in the heart, it followed, *first*, that the kingdom of God was moral, not nationalistic; *second*, that the kingdom of God was spiritual, not material; *third*, that the kingdom of God was actual, not ideal.

(1) *It is moral, not nationalistic.* Jesus told His fellow-countrymen bluntly that they had mistaken their enemy. They thought their enemy was Rome, the foreign legions that went marching up and down the highways of the land they loved. Jesus told them that the enemy whom they ought to fear and fight was the devil, the legions of evil that go marching through the sanctities of the soul. Again and again He came back to that. 'How can one enter into a strong man's house', He said, 'and spoil his goods, except he first bind the strong man? Then he will spoil his house' (Matt. xii, 29). Who was the 'strong man' Jesus was thinking of there? Not Caesar—but Satan. And Jesus added that if, up and down the land, broken lives were being healed and devils cast out, it was a sign that He, the Christ of God, had already bound the strong man, that the kingdom of Satan was now breaking up, and the kingdom of God coming into its own. But never did Jesus make this clearer than when He stood before Pilate. 'My kingdom is not of this world,' He said. 'If My kingdom were of this world, then would My servants fight; but now is My kingdom not from hence' (John xviii, 36). And it is one of history's most curious anomalies that whereas Rome, acting in the person of Pilate, crucified Jesus ostensibly at least because she could not allow the setting up of any rival earthly kingdom, and it was represented that that was what Jesus was seeking to do, the Jews, on the other hand, crucified Jesus because they did want passionately to see an earthly kingdom set up, and knew now that that was the one thing Jesus was determined *not* to do. 'My kingdom is not of this world'—that signed the death-warrant of Jewish nationalism, but it signed Jesus' death-warrant too. 'Away with Him,' they cried, 'this King who will not rule!' But Christ's rule, which is God's rule, is in the heart. It is in the secret places of a man's moral life. The kingdom, said Jesus, is moral, not nationalistic.

(2) *It is spiritual, not material.* It was not only an earthly kingdom on which the Jews had set their hearts. It was also an age of material good things. God's kingdom would lift them out of want and struggle, and set them down amongst the good things of this life.

Now you will remember that there was actually a point in Jesus' life when He considered the possibility of making use of that material hope in God's service. 'Make the stones bread!' said the Tempter. 'Appeal to men along the lower line first, and then they will be ready for the higher. Start by making them comfortable, and then they will have an ear for the Gospel.' But Jesus turned that suggestion down. All that, He said, would only obscure His message and complicate His challenge. For the kingdom of God was not meat and drink, but righteousness, and peace, and joy in the Holy Ghost (Rom. xiv, 17).

Translated into terms of today, this means that all the social reform in the world, *taken by itself*, will never bring in the kingdom; that there is a primary and essential work of God's grace in the inner man for which no amount of amelioration of his outward circumstances can possibly act as a substitute; that you will never make a Utopia out of regenerate conditions but unregenerate hearts, nor build the City of God out of men who have never been converted and redeemed. Admittedly, true religion has mighty social reactions, and it is those who have themselves found God who will be the first to join every crusade for the betterment of human conditions: get the spiritual side of things right, and you will assuredly be helping to put the material side right. (On this, see the Lesson on 'Jesus and Social Questions', pp. 132 ff). But the fact we have been insisting on remains. 'The kingdom', said Jesus, 'cometh not with observation. It is within you' (Luke xvii, 20 f), meaning, 'It is now in your midst, in the new age God is inaugurating.'

(3) *It is actual, not ideal.* The Jews could only dream of the kingdom: Jesus said it was already here. They could only cast longing eyes into a dim, ideal future: Jesus said it had arrived on earth, and was a present reality. One Sabbath in

4761

the synagogue of His home-town of Nazareth He read aloud
to the assembled people the great prophecy of Isaiah in which
the blessed coming of the kingdom was forecast—how the
broken-hearted would be healed, the captives delivered, the
blind given their sight; and then, closing the book, He
began—'This day is this fulfilled in your ears!' (Luke iv,
17 ff). And another day when talking in private to His
disciples, 'Blessed', He said, 'are the eyes which see the
things that ye see'—things for which kings and prophets of
old times yearned, and peered down the dark future, and
strained their eyes to see, and yet never saw—but ye see
them, the splendours of the kingdom! (Luke x, 23 f). Again
and again in the Gospels, Jesus strikes home to men's hearts
with this amazing discovery that the kingdom they dream
about has in some sense arrived, is here now for those whose
eyes are open and whose spiritual vision is cleansed. The
kingdom, said Jesus, is actual, not ideal.

'Where is the Church,' cried one of the gallant Scots
Covenanters in the persecuting days when the flock of Christ
was scattered over moor and glen, 'where is the Church of
God in Scotland at this day? I will tell you where the Church
is. It is wherever a praying young man or woman is at a
dykeside in Scotland: that's where the Church is.' So if we
ask, Where is the kingdom of God today? here is the Gospel
answer: it is wherever a man or woman has made Christ the
Lord of life and accepted the rule of God in the heart. That
is where the kingdom is. And that is the real explanation of
the sudden happiness that comes to any man who makes the
great decision: it is the other world, the eternal kingdom
world, breaking through into time, coming above the surface in that man's life. The kingdom of God is there.

4. *The Kingdom as the Rule of God in the World*

There was a second main line along which Christ's thought
of the kingdom ran. It was the rule of God in the heart; but
it was also *the rule of God in the world*. Here, again, Christ was
drawing three great distinctions. If the kingdom was the
rule of God in the world, it followed, *first*, that the kingdom

of God was social, not individualistic; *second*, that the kingdom of God was universal, not local; *third*, that the kingdom of God was awaiting a final consummation, and not yet fully complete.

(1) *It is social, not individualistic.* The very name implies that. It was to be a *kingdom*. It might indeed have its roots in solitary, separate souls that had been redeemed (religion always has its roots there), but its aim was nothing less than a redeemed society, a new order of humanity, a family fellowship, the sons and daughters of God. As this was Christ's programme and manifesto, it follows (and the united testimony of the Gospels makes this clear) that any religion which consists merely or mainly in getting one's own soul saved, which begins and ends in that, is something quite different from Christ's religion, something far inferior to Christ's religion, which never countenanced individualism run riot or the parochialism of a self-centred salvation. If there is a place in Christianity for desperate concern about one's own soul (and most certainly there is), there is also a place for this:

> I will not cease from mental fight,
> > Nor shall my sword sleep in my hand,
> Till we have built Jerusalem
> > In England's green and pleasant land.

The kingdom, said Jesus, is the rule of God in the world: it is social, not individualistic.

(2) *It is universal, not local.* 'The field is the world,' said Jesus, describing the ground on which the Gospel seed was to be sown (Matt. xiii, 38). Again, telling His men of their high responsibility as Christians, He said, 'Ye are the salt'— of what? Not of the Church, not of their own families, not of any one class or sect or party—'Ye are the salt of the earth'! (Matt. v, 13). And again, describing the magnetic force of the evangel with which they were charged—'They shall come from the east, and from the west, and from the north, and from the south, and shall sit down in the kingdom of God' (Luke xiii, 29). Never did Jesus think of God's

c

kingdom as an ark of refuge for the few, to which they could escape with a sigh of relief from a ruined world. Jesus came, not to snatch a few elect souls out of a lost and hopeless world: He came to save the world. Hence any Church which is content to minister to the few who are saved already, to carry them at last safe to their desired haven, and just leave all the rest, is definitely failing Christ. The Church is here, under Christ, to claim nothing less than the whole world for God's kingdom; and all the spiritual forces of the unseen are backing up the men who are pledged to that mighty imperialism. The kingdom, said Jesus, is universal, not local.

(3) *The Kingdom awaits a final consummation, and is not yet complete.* Here is the great paradox of it, that it is both present and future; present because (as we have seen) it is there now wherever there is a fully surrendered heart, but also future, because the crowning glory is still to come. 'When the Son of Man shall come in His glory', said Jesus, looking past the present order of things to some terrific act of God that would usher in the consummation, 'then shall the King say, Come, ye blessed of My Father, inherit the kingdom' (Matt. xxv, 31 ff). And whatever else that mighty Second Advent hope that glowed and blazed in Jesus' soul may mean, we know that at least it does mean this—that when man has done everything that man can do to build the everlasting kingdom, it is God, and God alone, who can make that kingdom perfect; that somehow and somewhere, in ways beyond our present comprehension, God is going to come breaking in triumphantly; that the age-long warfare between good and evil is not to drag on and on indefinitely as an indecisive warfare, but that one day it is going to end, and end in the victory of God, and on that day the last enemy will be dead beneath Christ's feet for ever. That was the winning note that Jesus struck. That was the eternal hope He gave the world, signed with His own name and guarantee. That was what generated the great vision of the seer with whose book the New Testament closes (Rev. xi, 15), the vision of a day when heaven itself would ring with a mighty tumult of voices, and their adoring, rejoicing cry

would be this—'The kingdoms of this world are become the kingdom of our Lord, and of His Christ; and He shall reign for ever and ever.'

7: THE FIRST TWELVE

1. *The Youth of the Disciples*

Christianity began as a young people's movement. In thinking of Jesus and His disciples, that is the first fact to make quite clear. Unfortunately, it is a fact which Christian art and Christian preaching have too often obscured. But it is quite certain that the original disciple band was a young men's group. Most of the Apostles were probably still in their twenties when they went out after Jesus.

In this connexion, notice how St. Paul, writing almost a generation later, reports that of the five hundred to whom the risen Christ appeared 'the greater part remain unto this present' (1 Cor. xv, 6): the natural inference is that the spiritual conquests of Jesus had been mainly among the younger people. Note also in the Gospels themselves the Master's forms of address to His followers. We find the Greek word *tekna*, meaning 'children', and sometimes the affectionate diminutive *teknia* (John xiii. 33), or *paidia* (John xxi, 5), 'my dear children', or as we might put it today (Dr Moffatt so translates it) 'lads'.

Jesus Himself, we should never forget, went out to His earthly ministry with 'the dew of His youth' upon Him (Ps. cx, 3—this Psalm was applied to Jesus, first by Himself, and then by the Apostolic Church). It was a true instinct that led the Christians of a later day, when they drew the likeness of their Master on the walls of the catacombs, to portray Him, not old and weary and broken with pain, but as a young shepherd out on the hills of the morning. The original version of Isaac Watts' great hymn was true to fact:

> When I survey the wondrous Cross,
> Where *the young Prince* of glory died.

And no one has ever understood the heart of youth, in its gaiety and gallantry and generosity and hope, its sudden loneliness and haunting dreams and hidden conflicts and strong temptations, no one has understood it nearly so well as Jesus. And no one ever realized more clearly than Jesus did that the adolescent years of life, when strange dormant thoughts are stirring and the whole world begins to unfold, are God's best chance with the soul. When Jesus and youth come together, deep calls to deep. There is an immediate, instinctive feeling of kinship, and everything that is fine and noble and pure in youth bows down in admiration and adoration before Him.

It is not surprising, then, that Christianity entered the world as a young people's movement. When we study the story of the first Twelve, it is a young men's adventure we are studying. We see them following their Leader out into the unknown, not knowing very clearly who He is, or why they are doing it, or where He is likely to lead them; but just magnetized by Him, fascinated and gripped and held by something irresistible in the soul of Him, laughed at by friends, plotted against by foes, with doubts sometimes growing clamorous in their own hearts, until they almost wished they were well out of the whole business; but still clinging to Him, coming through the ruin of their hopes to a better loyalty, and earning triumphantly at last the great name the *Te Deum* gives them, 'The glorious company of the Apostles'. It is worth watching them, for we too may catch the infection of their spirit, and fall into step with Jesus.

2. *Diversity of Character*

One of the most striking features of the first disciple-group was the diversity of character it contained. It was an amazing synthesis of humanly irreconcilable elements. Isaiah's vision of the wolf and the lamb dwelling together was surely near fulfilment when Simon the Zealot, the fiery nationalist, went arm-in-arm with Matthew, the tax-gatherer and publican! Only one thing could explain that strange union: they had each found Jesus. Here was Peter, all energy and activity and impetuosity, and here was John, meditative and thoughtful and prayerful. That difference, too, was transcended: they had each found Jesus. Here was Andrew, a man of shining, untroubled faith, and here was Thomas, with constitutional melancholy haunting him. They, too, were one now: they had each found Jesus. The very composition of that first group of twelve is a mighty witness to the universality of Christ.

In this point of diversity of character, the first group was a microcosm of the Church that was to be. 'I, if I be lifted up from the earth, will draw all men unto Me,' said Jesus (John xii, 32). He has done it, and is doing it—drawing men of every generation and century, for Jesus alone never goes out of date: men of every race and country, so that even Kipling's unbridgeable gulf between East and West is in Christ Jesus bridged once for all; men of every calling and vocation; men of every temperament and disposition; men of every class and party; men as diverse as Francis of Assisi and John Bunyan, John Wesley and John Henry Newman, Brother Lawrence and Aggrey of Africa, D. L. Moody and Temple Gairdner. The City of God, says Revelation, has gates facing to every point of the compass (xxi, 13): and they all lead in to Christ.

3. *The Master's Twofold Aim*

What was Jesus' purpose in selecting these men for special discipleship? St. Mark has put it into one short, significant sentence. 'He ordained twelve, that they should be with

Him, and that He might send them forth to preach' (Mark iii, 14). That sentence is worth pondering. 'That they should be with Him'—that suggests, does it not, that Jesus, on the human side of His nature, felt the need of human fellowship and sympathy? The Gospels are full of lonely people, the Virgin Mary, the friendless lepers, the man at the pool of Bethesda, Judas, Pilate, and many another; but in a sense the loneliest figure of all on the Gospel page is the Christ Himself. And often when the world outside had been showing itself callous and hostile and contemptuous, often when the day had brought Him sneers that stung, or a studied indifference that was like a blow in the face, He would turn back at nightfall with a great relief to these twelve men who, for all their faults and bungling, did love Him and did believe in Him. As Jesus Himself expressed it, one day when the end was near—'It is you who have stood by Me through My trials' (Luke xxii, 28, Moffatt). And still today the love and trust of ordinary people mean more to Jesus than we might ever guess. 'If any man open the door, I will come in.'

'That they should be with Him.' It was not only that the Saviour felt the need of human love and sympathy. It was also His purpose to train these men by fellowship with Himself. Living with Him every day, watching Him in all kinds of situations, listening to His private talk, being admitted to His dreams and aspirations and hopes, they would end by sharing His very spirit, would gradually come to see things with His eyes, and understand with His wonderfully understanding heart, and be fired with His own authentic fire. In short, the fellowship would make them real men of God. It is the best and simplest way of making real men and women of God today. Intimacy with Jesus is the best of all teachers.

'And that He might send them forth to preach.' The work in Galilee was growing so rapidly, and the opportunity was so great, and the need of perishing souls so desperate that Jesus could not keep the work of evangelization in His own hands. The twelve men were chosen to carry and to pass on the torch that Jesus had kindled. That is one reason why we call the Church 'the Body of Christ'.

For Christ has no hands but our hands to do His work today,
He has no feet but our feet to lead men in His way,
He has no tongue but our tongues to tell men how He died,
He has no help but our help to bring them to His side.

The word 'apostle' means 'one who is sent forth'; and no
man can be a true 'disciple' who is not prepared to be an
'apostle' too. Christ counts on you. Nineteen hundred years
ago a group of young people under Christ changed the
world. He is counting on young men and women today to do
it again. 'Let no man', said Martin Luther, 'lose the faith
that God willeth to do a great work through him.'

4. The Master's Call

How were the first twelve recruits enrolled? No doubt to
each of them the final call when it came was quite sudden
and abrupt and decisive, but it seems likely that in every case
a longer or shorter period of acquaintance with Jesus, and
even companionship, had gone before and prepared the way.
Indeed, there were probably three stages on the road to full
apostleship. To begin with, they were simply His friends,
remaining in their own homes and at their various secular
activities, but seeing Him and speaking with Him from time
to time. The second stage came with the sundering of home
ties and the relinquishing of ordinary occupations. Finally,
there came the day when from the main body of the followers
who had gathered round Him twelve were set apart for the
closest intimacy and the most vital work. The call to apostleship was then complete.

The apparent duplicating in the Gospels of the accounts
of the calling of the disciples has often been felt to be a problem. But the above explanation provides a solution. Thus,
for example, when we find one account of Peter's call in
John i, 42, another quite different account in Luke v, 10 f,
and still another in Mark iii, 13-16, it is not necessary to say
that only one of the three narratives can be authentic and
that the others must be eliminated. The fact is that they all
have a true place in the story. For each represents a distinct
stage in Peter's progress from his first acquaintance with

Jesus to his full surrender. It was really a threefold call, first the call to friendship, then the call to following, and finally the call to the full ministry of apostleship.

5. *The Twelve Men*

Look now at some of the men Jesus chose. One of them, Andrew, has become Scotland's patron saint. Whether the legends connecting Andrew and Scotland have any truth in them or not we do not know: what we do know is that Scotland has a patron saint of whom she may well be proud. Andrew is a Greek word meaning brave, or manly, and the name describes the man. It was anything but an easy part Andrew had to play in the Gospel story. You will observe that he is generally described as 'Simon Peter's brother', and it is not an easy thing to be continually eclipsed by someone's else brilliance, and to have to stand in the shadow, even when that someone else is a brother. Andrew found Jesus before Peter: without Andrew, there might never have been a Peter in Christian history at all. Yet he had to stand and see Peter admitted to an intimacy (the inmost circle consisted of Peter, James, and John), which he was never privileged to share. It was a real test of the man. And he came through with flying colours. Andrew had not one particle of envy in his whole nature.

Andrew was one of the young men who had been deeply stirred by John the Baptist's revival movement. Indeed, it was through that movement that he was first brought into contact with Jesus. 'Behold the Lamb of God,' the Baptist had said, pointing to Someone walking one evening alone by the river (John i, 36). And Andrew and his friend, not knowing why they did it, went after that solitary figure. 'Where dwellest Thou?' 'Come and see.' And what would we not have given for a record of the conversation in that humble lodging that night, when Jesus and these two young men were alone together from four in the afternoon to dusk, and from dusk to dark, and from dark to the late, deep hour when the candles were at last put out! At any rate, after that, Andrew was Christ's man through and through.

It is an exceedingly significant fact that wherever Andrew appears on the Gospel scene he is busy introducing someone else to Jesus. It began the very next morning, when he broke in on his brother Simon with that glad 'Eureka! I have found the Christ!' 'And he brought him to Jesus' (John i, 42). When a famished crowd had followed the Master into the desert, it was Andrew who found the lad with the loaves (John vi, 8 f): and he brought him to Jesus. When the Greek strangers appealed to Philip for an introduction to his Master, it was to Andrew that Philip went for advice (John xii, 20-22): and he brought them to Jesus. Andrew is not only the patron saint of Scotland. He is the patron saint of all missionary workers for ever. And that is still the disciple's calling—to bring someone else to Christ.

Peter was a born leader and the natural spokesman of the disciple-group. When Jesus, watching the crowds dwindling put the question, 'Will ye also go away?' it was Peter who burst out with, 'Lord, to whom shall we go? Thou hast the words of eternal life' (John vi, 68). When the first great Christian confession came, it was Peter who made it: 'Thou art the Christ, the Son of the living God' (Matt. xvi, 16). When the broken-hearted band reassembled after Calvary, it was Peter who took the initiative. 'I go a fishing.' 'We also go with thee' (John xxi, 3). Gallant, generous-hearted, affectionate, impetuous soul that he was, he was a born leader of men.

But he had the defects of his qualities. It was to Peter that 'Get thee behind Me, Satan' was said (Matt. xvi, 23). It was Peter who blurted out his mercenary question, 'Behold, we have forsaken all, and followed Thee; what shall we have therefore?' (Matt. xix, 27). It was Peter who disowned Christ at the gibe of a servant-lass (Matt. xxvi, 69 ff). What a moral mixture the human heart can be! Peter's story is quite familiar. It is our story too.

Yet 'Peter', Christ's name for Simon, means 'the Rock'. Jesus was looking into the future and seeing the mighty man of God that His bungling disciple was going to be. And what really turned Peter from shifting sand into a rock was the discovery that after his tragic failure Jesus believed in him still (Mark xvi, 7). 'Thou knowest all things; Thou knowest that I love Thee.' 'Feed My sheep' (John xxi, 17).

A famous legend of Peter's last days at Rome has come to us. Fleeing from the city in sudden panic, he met Jesus entering. 'Quo vadis, Domine?' ('Whither goest Thou, Master?') he asked. 'I go to Rome to be crucified a second time for thee,' was the answer. Whereupon Peter turned and went back with firm step to the martyr-death awaiting him. And so this 'Mr Valiant' of the early Church crossed the river. 'And all the trumpets sounded for him on the other side.'

In the inner circle of Christ's followers were the two sons of Zebedee, James and John. About James little is known. Only in two incidents in the Gospel does he appear, and both times it is in his brother's company. But his ineffaceable title to honour lies in this, that he was the protomartyr of the apostolic band (see Acts xii, 2). John we may call the Jonathan of the New Testament: what Jonathan was to David in the Old Testament, that was John to the great Son of David in the New, 'My knights', says Tennyson's Arthur, 'are sworn to vows of utter hardihood, utter gentleness': and in John that manly strength and womanly tenderness seem to have been perfectly united. It stands eternally to John's credit that he was there on Calvary to the last, and that it was of him that the words fell from Jesus' dying lips, 'Woman, behold thy son!' (John xix, 26). No doubt there was another side to his nature, too, a less pleasing side, which comes out in three Gospel incidents—his rebuke to the unknown healer (Mark ix, 38), his threat of fire to the recalcitrant Samaritan village (Luke ix, 54), and his ambition for the best place in the kingdom (Mark x, 35 ff). But the deepest thing in his nature was his passionate love for Jesus that was like a flame in his heart. And wherever the Gospel is preached, one great name, 'the disciple whom Jesus loved', will be told for a memorial of him.

One disciple to whom something less than full justice has been done by history is Thomas. He is generally called Thomas the Doubter, or the Agnostic, or even the Sceptic.

That is hardly fair. It is worth remembering that when Jesus was setting His face towards Jerusalem and most of the disciples were protesting loudly against what seemed to them sheer reckless folly (John xi, 8), one brave, quiet voice spoke up—'Let us also go, that we may die with Him' (John xi, 16). If doubts did overshadow his soul (John xiv, 5; xx, 25), they were certainly not the doubts of defiant scepticism. Rather were they just the penalty of his temperament, in which a touch of melancholy was mingled. And it is a great thing that in the end the finest confession of faith in the New Testament comes from this soul that fought its way through the mists and shadows to the light—'My Lord and my God' (John xx, 28).

Matthew was 'sitting at the receipt of custom' when Jesus called him (Matt. ix, 9). To be a *publicanus*, or a tax-gatherer, was to be hopelessly branded and stigmatized in the eyes of every loyal Jew; and the surprise in Capernaum that night must have been great when it was rumoured who the Rabbi's latest recruit was. This was the kind of friendship by which Jesus, to quote St. Paul's words, 'made Himself of no reputation' (Phil. ii, 7). But what matter? Neither Matthew nor Jesus recked anything of what the crowd might say. That very night Matthew gave a feast to all his friends (and a strange company they would be), with Jesus as his guest of honour (Matt. ix, 10). Probably the converted tax-gatherer had three main motives in giving the feast. It was to celebrate his spiritual birthday; it was to provide an opportunity for an open confession of his new allegiance, a confession which would mean committing himself publicly and irrevocably to Jesus and burning his boats behind him, so that there could be no going back to the old life; and it was to give his friends a chance of meeting Jesus and sharing his own wonderful experience. The name 'Friend of publicans and sinners' was first flung at Christ as a gibe; but it is His crowning glory now.

Little is known of five of the remaining six disciples, namely, Philip, the earnest inquirer (see especially John i, 43 ff; xiv, 8 f); Simon, the Zealot and fiery nationalist; Bartholomew, who is probably to be identified with Nathanael (John i, 45 ff); Lebbaeus, 'whose surname was Thaddaeus' (Matt. x, 3), who also had the name Judas (not Iscariot), and who is known to us by one single remark (John xiv, 22); and James the son of Alphaeus, of whom nothing at all is told. There remains only the dark enigma of the group, Judas Iscariot, 'who also betrayed Him'. We cannot enter into the problem of Judas here. Suffice it to say that Jesus must have seen in Judas at one time the makings of a real apostle, else He would never have chosen him; and that Judas must have been attracted and fascinated by Jesus, else he would never have left all to follow Him. We shall try to probe the mystery of Judas in a later study (see pp. 164ff).

These twelve men, then, Jesus chose, and with them set out to conquer the earth. An absurd adventure? Humanly speaking, yes. But God was in it. And 'God hath chosen the weak things of the world, to confound the things which are mighty; and base things of the world, and things which are despised, hath God chosen, yea, and things which are not, to bring to nought things that are' (1 Cor. i, 27 f).

8: THE TEACHING METHOD OF JESUS

1. *Jesus as Teacher*

When Nicodemus came to Jesus by night, he opened the conversation with the words, 'We know that Thou art *a teacher come from God*' (John iii, 2); and history has echoed his verdict. The teaching of Jesus, even though great multitudes throughout the world are still outside its sphere, even though many of His own followers have never cared or never dared to put it fully into practice, has had a power and an effect with which the influence of no other teacher can even for a moment be compared. He stands alone—the Great Teacher. Readers of the Gospels cannot but be impressed by the large proportion of His time and strength which Jesus deliberately dedicated to the ministry of teaching. Clearly, then, it is of the utmost importance that we should study the teaching method of Jesus. How did He frame His lessons? How did He make contact with His hearers? How did He present His truths? How did He get His results? Questions like these are vital not only in view of the remarkable interest in the question of teaching methods in general at the present time, and the thoroughgoing revolution in method which recent years have witnessed: quite apart from that, they open up for us a new window into the mind of the Master Himself.

It is necessary, however, in speaking of the teaching method of Jesus, to make, right at the outset, two qualifications. First, the word 'method' must not here be taken as suggesting a carefully enunciated and formulated system. The leading feature of all Jesus' teaching was its spontaneity and freedom. It was above all rules. And second, let us never forget that while Jesus was a teacher, a born teacher and a Prince of teachers, He was also far more than a teacher. It is no exaggeration to say, and it cannot be too strongly put, that if we possessed the whole bulk of Jesus' New Testament teaching, *and nothing more than that*, the world to-day would still be perishing as surely as if He had never come. For He Himself is far more than His teaching; and it is not the teaching of Christ that saves, but the Christ who teaches. Dr Dale was right on the mark when he said very memorably that Jesus came not so much to preach the Gospel as rather that there might be a Gospel to preach.

But keeping these two considerations in mind, we can now face our subject. For the sake of clearness, let us follow two lines of inquiry. What were the particular features of Jesus' teaching method? And what were its general principles?

2. *The Particular Features of Jesus' Teaching Method*

The first feature to be noticed is a very obvious one: *it was oral teaching*. It was spoken, not written. Indeed, only once in the Gospels do we see Jesus writing, and then it was in the sand He wrote (John viii, 6). All His precious, golden words, all His final pronouncements on faith and morals, all His 'oracles of God', were trusted to the memories of a group of Galilean peasants and fisherfolk.

Was it not a risk? Was there not a danger that the winds of the years might carry His words away, and all He had taught be lost? No. For Jesus knew (and in many a parable He came back to this) that once you have planted a seed, you can leave it to look after itself: God and the soil will do the rest. He knew that once He had planted His words in human hearts, He could confidently leave them there: they would haunt men down the years, and would live for ever. No need for Him to write His teaching down; that teaching, once let loose upon the earth, would make its way by its own inherent power and march deathlessly across the ages.

Ibsen, in his *Emperor and Galilean*, puts a soliloquy into the fourth-century Emperor Julian's mouth. 'Where is He now? Has He been at work elsewhere since *that* happened at Golgotha? Where is He now? What if He goes on and on, suffers and dies and conquers again and again, from world to world?' That has been the story of the words of Jesus.

A second notable feature of Jesus' method lies in the fact that *much of His profoundest teaching was elicited by quite casual incidents and events*. That is to say, it was largely unpremeditated, aimed at the particular circumstances of the moment, and addressed to a specific situation. An encounter with a paralytic in the synagogue (Matt. xii, 10), a wayside interview with a young aristocrat (Matt. xix, 16), a sudden quarrel among His disciples (Luke ix, 46), a debate on the vexed question of the imperial taxation (Matt. xxii, 17)— these are instances of the particular situations out of which much of the Master's teaching arose.

Now it might be thought that teaching like this was bound to be purely local and temporal in its application, and therefore not valid for us today. Nothing could be further from the truth. In point of fact, it is precisely because so much of Jesus' teaching was of that apparently incidental nature, addressed directly to the passing needs of the moment, that it does still hold good. Anything systematic in the way of doctrine or philosophy would, no doubt, have perished long ago; but these flashing words, because they struck straight home to the urgent needs of the actual men and women whom Jesus met and talked with, remain valid for ever. Systems of thought are continually changing from age to age, but the human heart, with its problems and perplexities, does not change; and human temptations today are still as tempting, and human tears as bitter, as when Satan whispered in Simon Peter's soul or Mary Magdalene wept at Jesus' feet. It is because Christ spoke to immediate, definite needs that His teaching now belongs to all the world.

A third feature to be noticed is this: *always Jesus' teaching was adapted to His audience.* The first thing He did was to put Himself at the point of view of His hearers, and to start from that. Was the law of Moses their working religion? Then with the law of Moses Jesus would begin, and go on from that to the better law of God. Was it a national kingdom they were dreaming of for Israel? Then Jesus would meet them on that ground, and lead them on to a spiritual kingdom. Always He began where His hearers were.

Hence the wonderful simplicity of His language. Direct and simple and forceful, that language—so unlike the speech of the professional religion of His day—had a grip and an appeal from which men could not get away. And He never went too fast. He never rushed His pupils. Step by step He led them. 'I have yet many things to say unto you,' He once told them, 'but ye cannot bear them now' (John xvi, 12). With divine reserve and reticence He would keep back part of the revelation (His own Sonship of God, for example) until His hearers were able to receive it.

The practical issue of this for today ought to be stressed. It never was Christ's way to demand a full-fledged faith for a beginning. It never was His way to hold men back from discipleship on the ground of an incomplete creed. And quite certainly that is not His way today. He puts Himself alongside His brethren. He bids them attach themselves to Him at any point they can. He takes them on with the faith that they can offer Him. He is content with that as a beginning; and from that He leads His friends on, as He led the first group on, step by step, to the inmost secret of who He is, and to the full glory of discipleship.

One other particular feature of His method is very apparent, namely, *the figurative element in His teaching.* By His illustrations, His epigrams, His paradoxes, and above all, by His parables, those matchless pictures which are not only creations of purest artistry but also living revelations of grace, windows opening suddenly upon life and destiny and God, He made men actually *see* the truths which He was proclaiming. Very often, while Jesus was speaking, some sudden picture would flash its way across His hearers' minds, so that even those whom no amount of abstract reasoning or argument would have convinced were left crying, 'I see it! I see it!' Many were ready to confess that until they met Jesus they had been blind, drifting through life like men with eyes shut, more than half asleep, never guessing at life's glory; but that now, thanks to Him, they were awake and alive, seeing life and seeing God. Jesus was the world's great giver of *vision*.

3. *The General Principles of Jesus' Teaching Method*

Turning now from the particular features of Jesus' method to its general principles, we notice, first that *it was authoritative teaching*. 'The people', says Matthew, 'were astonished at His doctrine, for He taught them as one having authority, and not as the scribes' (Matt. vii, 28 f). With Jesus, there was no 'perhaps', or 'it may be so', or 'I rather think so', no speculation or guesswork or fumbling or faltering, but 'Verily I say unto you' rung out with the assurance of God Himself. 'Not as the scribes'—for the scribes relied slavishly on tradition, 'Thus saith Moses', 'Thus saith Rabbi X', 'Thus saith the law and the prophets', never daring to speak in their own name. In other words, it was all second-hand religion. And the fact that it was second-hand could not be hid. Even the common people who listened to them knew it was second-hand, and felt the unreality of it, and despised it in their hearts. What Emerson says of Seneca might well be applied to the scribes, 'His thoughts are excellent if only he had the right to utter them,' for they were talking of things they had never experienced. But into that there burst this new voice out of Galilee—'It was said by them of old time . . . but I say unto you'—with one stroke sweeping scribism and all its buttressed positions aside, striking down through all the layers of tradition to bedrock fact, to the living God. And men were left gasping at the sheer daring of it, amazed and over-whelmed by the marvellous assurance of it, but also feeling with a great thrill of the heart that here was the real thing at last, here was a Man who had seen what He was talking about, and knew it and had a right to speak, a Man straight from God!

It should be stressed that here again we are dealing with something not local and temporal in its significance, but universal and permanent. Our own age, which has seen the breaking up of so many old and cherished traditions and the issuing of a new challenge to authority in so many spheres—in morals and religion, no less than in politics and society—is not, as some would suggest, left without chart or compass: *the Christ still stands*. To heart, and mind, and conscience His teaching still authenticates itself as the authoritative voice of God.

But notice, second, that although Jesus' teaching was authoritative, *it was never in any overbearing sense didactic or dogmatic or forcing assent*. Continually, as you turn the pages of the Gospels, one fact stares out at you—the quite amazing patience of Jesus with the men He had to teach, His steadfast refusal to compel them or dictate to them or bend them to His will, His overwhelming respect for their personalities. Why was He so sparing with His miraculous powers? Because He had no wish to dazzle men's minds or override their calmer judgement. Why did He take the risk, after the Twelve had been only a comparatively short time with Him, of sending them out to preach? Partly, at least, it was in order that they might be free to verify things for themselves, free to test, out in the whirl of life, whether what He had been giving them would really work. The keynote of all Jesus' teaching of His disciples was, 'I call you not servants, but I have called you friends' (John xv, 15); and if that keynote had been remembered, His followers of a later day could never have fallen (as they have sometimes fallen) into the mistake of trying to stifle thought by loading men with infallible dogmas demanding implicit assent. 'Not slaves, but friends,' said Jesus. Not—'There is the truth:

accept it, or perish!' but 'I am the truth: live with Me, and you will find it.' 'If any man will do His will, he shall know of the doctrine' (John vii, 17). His teaching was authoritative always, overbearing and dogmatic never.

Closely related to this profound respect for men's personalities is a third great principle of Jesus' method, namely, *His determination to make men think for themselves*. This is a main part of every true teacher's work. If the teacher fails in this, he fails altogether. Now Jesus by His teaching gave the greatest stimulus to thought and questioning the world has ever experienced. Indeed, in one sense it would be true to say that it was far more Christ's purpose to stimulate interest than to supply answers. Notice, for instance, how often He refused to give a direct answer to a direct question. 'Who is my neighbour?' a lawyer once asked Him; and the answer was, 'A certain man went down to Jericho'—that, and a story (Luke x, 29 ff). 'Lord, and what shall this man do?' said Peter, pointing to John. 'What is that to thee? Follow thou Me' (John xxi, 21 f). 'Lord, are there few that be saved?' asked another. 'Strive to enter in!' (Luke xiii, 23 f). And all the parables had that for their aim—to make men use their own powers of spiritual insight and perception upon spiritual realities. 'Thou shalt love the Lord thy God', said Jesus, quoting Deuteronomy, 'with all thy *mind*' (Mark xii, 30). And again, 'He that hath ears to hear, let him hear' (Matt. xi, 15, etc.), which simply means, Use the spiritual powers God has given you!

Hence we see that it was, and is, no part of the purpose of Jesus' teaching to supply ready-made answers to each and every problem of life. Problems in abundance there were and are, if He had cared to legislate on them, problems of Sabbath observance, religion and politics, master and man, and many more. But Jesus came to earth to be something better than a mechanical legislator. God was not incarnate amongst men to supply cut-and-dried solutions to all their difficulties. What the Master did aim at supplying, what He lived and died to supply, was a new and living spirit by whose light and strength men could face their problems victoriously and win their way through. As Paul puts it, 'The letter killeth, but the Spirit giveth life' (2 Cor. iii, 6). And this is the liberty with which Christ makes men free.

A fourth great principle of Jesus' method was the fact that *what He taught, He lived*. The disciples could never feel that there was anything vague or abstract or indefinite about their Master's teaching, for it was all being made concrete and personal before their eyes, all incarnate in Himself. Was it faith in God that was the lesson? How gloriously He lived that lesson out Himself! Was it the forgiving of injuries He was urging upon them? How whole-heartedly He Himself forgave! Was it the importance of prayer that He was teaching? He Himself prayed all the night long. He did not only speak to them of the necessity of service and self-sacrifice: He took a towel, and girded Himself, and washed their feet. He did not make orations about brotherhood: He went into the homes of the despised, and sat at their tables, and called them friends and brothers. Christ was the supreme Teacher, because He lived supremely what He taught, and lived it entirely non-professionally and naturally. In this He is an example for all His followers for ever. No man's religion will ever make any real impact on the world if the man is not putting himself into it, if he is not living it. But if he is, it may be irresistible anywhere.

The last great principle of Jesus' teaching to which we shall point is this—*His intimacy with and love for those He taught*. 'One loving spirit', said St. Augustine, 'sets another on fire'; and that was and is the ultimate secret of Christ's divine success as Teacher. From His loving spirit the spirits of His pupils were continually catching fire, so that the lesson, in that flame of mutual love, was no dreary discipline, but joy and romance and glory. Bungling pupils in Christ's school the disciples often were, disappointing Him sorely at a score of points and stumbling sadly over His great lesson of faith and hope and love. And yet, for all the sorry show they made in these things, their love to Him was growing all the time. His loving spirit was triumphing over all the hindrances in them. And a day came (it was after Calvary and Pentecost) when at long last they had their lesson—the great central message of redemption—perfect and complete and without any flaw at all; and went forth to proclaim it to the earth.

9: THE FATHERHOOD OF GOD

Mon.	Isa. lxiii, 9-16	The Vision of a Prophet
Tues.	Matt. xi, 25-30	The Father and the Son
Wed.	Mark iv, 35-41	Jesus' Faith in the Father
Thur.	Matt. vii, 7-11	The Lord will Provide
Fri.	Luke xv, 11-24	The Father's Love for the Lost
Sat.	Matt. xxiii, 1-12	
		God's Fatherhood and Man's Brotherhood
Sun.	Matt. vi, 9-15	The Family Prayer

Psalm ciii, 13-18: 'Such pity as a father hath'
Hymnary 547: 'Put thou thy trust in God'

1. *Revelation, not Argument*

It is a very striking fact that Jesus never argued for the existence of God. Search the Gospels from first to last for 'proofs' of God, and you will search in vain. Why?

One reason undoubtedly was this. Jesus knew that in those ultimate matters argument, taken by itself and apart from something higher, will never breed conviction. It may remove certain difficulties: it cannot beget vision. Omar Khayyam's experience is familiar:

> Myself when young did eagerly frequent
> Doctor and Saint, and heard great Argument
> About it and about; but evermore
> Came out by the same Door as in I went.

There were certain historic 'proofs' of the existence of God of which an older generation made much; but in point of fact it has never been, it is not now, and it never will be along that road that conviction comes and men get a grip of God. A living conviction is bred by two things, each of them higher and deeper than argument, namely, the direct action of God upon the soul—which is Revelation; and the response of the soul to that divine initiative—which is Faith.

75

Hence the Bible, which is psychologically as well as religiously the sanest book in the world, does not start off with—'Let us summarize the arguments for God,' or 'Now as to the question whether there exists a God or not,' or anything of the kind; but goes in one bold stride right to the heart of things with these great challenging words, like the sudden beat of a drum—'*In the beginning God.*' Hence Jesus, when He came, never stopped to prove God. He came to do something better than that. He came to reveal God.

In any case, there was no need to argue. He assumed a belief in God among His immediate hearers, and He was right to assume it. Jesus was a Jew, and His hearers were Jews, and the heart of the Jewish religion was a convinced monotheism. The essence of it was the Deuteronomic creed—'Hear, O Israel: The Lord our God is one Lord' (Deut. vi, 4). The belief in God was there already, and Jesus could count on it. So much at least was common ground between the Preacher and His hearers. On that basis He could go to work and build. Hence the question was not—'Is there a God?' It was—'Granted that there is a God, what is this God like?'

To that question Christ's answer was one constantly reiterated word—'Father'. Within the short compass of our Gospels, that name occurs more than one hundred and fifty times. It is there in the first recorded boyhood utterance of Jesus—'Wist ye not that I must be about My Father's business?' (Luke ii, 49). It is there in His last dying cry—'Father, into Thy hands I commend My spirit' (Luke xxiii, 46). Christendom, with the Gospels in its hands, has inevitably fixed on this as the supreme name for God for ever.

2. *The Original Element in Jesus' Teaching*

It would not, of course, be true to suppose that Jesus was the first to call God Father. Dimly and gropingly the men of the Old Testament had been feeling after this great thought on which Christ set His seal. To begin with they conceived of God's Fatherhood almost solely in the national sphere. He was the Father of the chosen people. 'Thus saith the

Lord,' said Moses to Pharaoh, 'Israel is My son, even My first-born' (Exod. iv, 22). That was a national Fatherhood. But already in the Old Testament you can see men's thoughts moving out to something deeper and more personal, especially in some of the Psalms, as, for example, when God is called the 'Father of the fatherless' (lxviii, 5), or in that word of wonderful compassion and beauty—'Like as a father pitieth his children, so the Lord pitieth them that fear Him' (ciii, 13). We cannot say that Jesus was the first to call God Father.

In what respects, then, was His teaching here original and new? In two respects.

He took this thought that had been a stray guest, hovering uncertainly on the dim borderland and circumference of men's minds, and *made it the centre of everything*. Before Jesus, many good people had thought of God's relationship to men mainly in terms of a Potter and his clay, or a Creator and his creatures, or a Dictator and his subjects. But to Jesus all these conceptions were dim half-lights, hiding as much as they revealed. The likest thing on earth to God's relationship to men, said Jesus, was the family relationship, the life of a father and his children. Now that new emphasis of Jesus, that centralizing of this conception, was something unheard of and revolutionary; and it changed the whole face of religion.

The other respect in which Jesus' thought of God as Father was completely original was *the new depth and content He put into the word*. For not only did He make the word central: He enriched it beyond recognition. And He did that not so much by anything He said, as by the way He lived. Jesus, alone in history, has lived out consistently and unbrokenly and shiningly and triumphantly the kind of life that a vital sense of the divine Fatherhood should imply. Here in this absolutely filial life of Christ, this perfect sonship of the Master, all the tenderness and strength and serenity and amazing everlasting dependableness of the Father-God are mirrored. So Jesus gave the word Father a depth of which men had never dreamed.

3. *The Meaning of Fatherhood*

Now the way is open for us to come to the heart of our subject. When Christ taught men to look up and call God Father what did He mean by it? What practical consequences did He draw? (Here, for the sake of clearness, we shall set down the various truths which Jesus' thought of Fatherhood contains, giving illustrative materials from the Gospels in each case; but in the actual teaching of the subject of this lesson, it will be found better to begin with the Gospel illustrations, and to lead on from these to the underlying principles.)

(1) Since God is a Father, said Jesus, *He is vitally interested in all His children's concerns.* Jesus asked the world to believe —and to believe with no 'ifs' or 'buts' or conditions, but radically and out-and-out—that even things like food and clothing are most certainly God's concern; that when 'man goeth forth unto his work, and to his labour, until the evening', God goes forth with him; and that, at the back of things, unseen and unrecognized often but everlastingly gracious, there is a loving heart thinking for His people all the time, planning for them, remembering them, arranging wonderful surprises of sheer goodness for them. Jesus put all that into one great, simple sentence, 'If ye then'—you fathers—'know how to give good gifts unto your children, how much more shall your Father which is in heaven give good things to them that ask Him?' (Matt. vii, 11).

Now Jesus did not only teach that faith. He lived it. He practised what He preached. Every page of the Gospels shows you Jesus taking the faith in a Father-God which He proclaimed to men and putting Himself into it, body and soul. Out of a great mass of instances, take just one (Mark iv, 37 ff). There was a night on the Galilean Lake when the sudden whirlwind blew and the waves were lashed to fury, and the frail fishing-craft sagged and struggled in the trough of the waves. The fishermen looked into one another's terrified faces and cried that this was the end. But Jesus lay asleep on a pillow. To us, reading the story today, that sleeping Christ in the storm is one of the most compelling arguments for faith in the world. Asleep—why? Because it was God's sea, and the waves and the wind and the dark were in His Father's hand, and underneath were the ever-lasting arms.

By teaching and life Jesus showed that to know a God who is thus vitally interested in all His children's concerns is to have the secret of a peace, a poise, and a steadiness that nothing in life can disturb. The man who has made that dis-covery has passed out of the bondage of fear and worry into a glorious liberty and release. He is a man who has achieved absolute independence of circumstances in utter dependence upon God. He has found what Jesus meant by 'blessedness' (Matt. v, 3 ff). He is doing what the New Testament calls 'overcoming the world'. Because God is at his right hand, he shall not be moved.

(2) Since God is a Father, said Jesus, *He knows and loves each individual soul*. A father does not love his family in general: he loves each child in particular. Even so, 'the very hairs of your head are all numbered' (Matt. x, 30). 'God so loved the world' (John iii, 16) is but one side of the shield: the other is this—'There is joy in the presence of the angels of God over *one* sinner that repenteth' (Luke xv, 10). The shepherd leaves the ninety-nine sheep in the fold, and goes out after the one (Luke xv, 4-7). Christ's own re-deeming work shows the individualizing love of God in action. Crowds surged round Jesus, but it was the single soul that engrossed and fascinated Him. There were scores of ailing folk at the Pool of Bethesda: Jesus went straight to the one poor, desperate soul who had had thirty-eight years of disappointment (John v, 2 ff). When the slow, sad pro-cession filed out from the gates of Nain, Jesus had eyes only for the weeping mother who had lost her boy (Luke vii, 11 ff). Pressed and jostled by a gaping crowd, He turned round and singled out the one shrinking soul who needed to touch Him most (Mark v. 25 ff). Some of the most glorious words in the Gospel were given first to one lonely woman who had bungled her life (John iv, 7 ff). He walked and talked with Nicodemus in the dark (John iii, 1 ff). He escaped from the Jericho crowd and chose Zacchaeus for

His host (Luke xix, 1 ff). Looking at Jesus, we feel the force of St. Augustine's dictum about God—'He loves us every one as though there were but one of us to love.'

(3) Since God is a Father, said Jesus, *men can be absolutely natural in their religion.* By bringing in the family conception, He struck a death-blow at that devastating thing, formality in religion. Men had been thinking that God could be satisfied only with pomp and ceremony (Matt. vi, 5; xxiii, 23); but that was not the way in which any earthly father wished his children to come to him, and certainly God the Father of heaven did not require it. That does not mean that we can be irreverent in our approach to God, or take liberties with Him who is God over all, blessed for ever. But it does mean that the barriers of formality are down. The veil is rent in twain from the top to the bottom, and the way to God lies open (Matt. xxvii, 51). One result of this is that simple petitionary prayer gains a new importance and authority. The idea that we should eliminate the element of definite petition from our prayers received no countenance from Jesus. If God is your Father, said Jesus, and you are His child, then clearly you can take all your requests and desires to Him (Matt. vii, 7 ff). It would be unnatural to refrain from taking them, and if anything in your relationship to God is unnatural it is wrong. By calling God Father, Jesus has baptized religion into a new freedom and liberty and childlike directness and simplicity.

(4) Since God is a Father, said Jesus, *pain has a meaning.* In the old days indeed (in many passages of the Old Testament, for instance) men were apt to think that pain, suffering, trials of all kinds were signs of an angry God's condemnation, judgements upon their sins. Sometimes that may be the truth, but certainly not invariably. Christ has cleared that awful thought away; and we know now that there are some kinds of suffering at least, which so far from being God's condemnation of a soul, can actually be experienced —through the gracious influence of the Spirit—as God's election of that soul for signal honour. (On the other aspect of suffering as an intruder in the world, something to be

challenged and removed, see the Lesson on 'The Ministry of Healing', pp. 94ff).

So it was with Jesus Himself. St. Paul, describing Jesus' sufferings, says 'God spared not His own Son' (Rom. viii, 32). Why was He not spared? Because God had a purpose for Him, a great and glorious world-redeeming purpose, and the suffering was the road to it. So God deals with all His children. 'Blessed are ye when men shall persecute you for My sake' (Matt. v, 11). As the writer to the Hebrews puts it, 'What son is he whom the father chasteneth not?' (Heb. xii, 7).

There is also another way in which the thought of God's Fatherhood lets in light on the problem of human pain. It implies that God shares in that pain Himself. For if God is a Father, and you are His child, it follows that any suffering you have to face in this world is His suffering too, that anything that hurts you hurts God (because He is a real Father) far more, and that any furnace of trouble you have to pass through is seven times heated for Him. 'In all their affliction He was afflicted' (Isa. lxiii, 9). The supreme instance of that is Calvary. On the green hill far away they raised the Cross, but the real Cross was in heaven, in the Father-heart of the Eternal.

(5) Since God is a Father, said Jesus, *sin and forgiveness stand in a new light.* On the one hand, sin grows darker. If the power behind the universe were sheer impersonal law, then our wrong thoughts and deeds would be sins against law. But if the power behind the universe is, as Jesus revealed, a Father, then our wrong thoughts and deeds are sins against love. And if it is bad to strike a blow at a fixed, rigid law, it is ten times worse to strike a blow at a loving heart. Indeed, to call God Father is ultimately to make sin intolerable. The greatest of all the parables, the story of the prodigal (Luke xv, 11 ff), drives that lesson home; but not content with teaching it Christ died to make it plain. For it was not law that men crucified on Calvary—it was God's holy love.

Crucified—but not killed! For at the Cross the Father-heart of God passed breaking-point and refused to break;

and if sin stands in a new light, so does love's victory over sin, which is forgiveness. Can God forgive? men asked before Jesus came, and the answer was always more or less in doubt. But call Him Father, and at once the question becomes—How can God *not* forgive? Daringly Jesus pictured God, not waiting for His shamed child to slink home, nor standing on His dignity when he came, but running out to gather him, shamed and ragged and muddied as he was, to His welcoming arms. The same name 'Father' has at once darkened the colour of sin and heightened the splendid glory of forgiveness. (This will be more fully treated in the Lesson on 'Sin and its Remedy', pp. 83 ff).

(6) Finally, since God is a Father, said Jesus, *all men are brothers*. Clearly no one has a right to take Jesus' words 'Our Father' upon his lips, no man is using the Lord's Prayer sincerely, who is not prepared to treat all men everywhere as members of the same family as himself. In an age that is clamorous about brotherhood, it is strange surely that we do not hear more of the one great conviction on which alone a lasting brotherhood can be built—the conviction of the divine Fatherhood. (See below, 'The Royal Law of Love', pp. 123 ff). When Jesus implanted that conviction in men's hearts, it was not only a law of brotherliness He was giving, but also an adequate motive. To be able to say of another, 'That man like myself has God for Father, he too is a child of God,' is to be well on the way to vanquish all unbrotherly feelings. Here, at least, the dictum that 'East is East, and West is West, and never the twain shall meet' breaks down; here divergences of temperament are transcended, and jarring prejudices give way; here denominationalism falls into true perspective, and all the rifts within the lute that spoil the spiritual music are healed; here the deep cleavages of race and nationality are bridged, and back of the United Nations something even grander, finer, nobler begins to come into view—the Family of God. Here, in Jesus' revelation of God as Father, the hope of a unified earth has been given once for all, the vision of the New Jerusalem coming down out of heaven, adorned as a bride for her husband.

10: SIN AND ITS REMEDY

Mon. Mark vii, 14-23   The Inwardness of Sin
Tues. Luke xxii, 39-44   What Sin costs Christ
Wed. Matt. xxv, 31-46   The Judgement of God
Thur. Mark ii, 1-12   Forgiveness embodied in Jesus
Fri. Luke xv, 1-10   The Joy of Forgiveness
Sat. Luke xix, 1-10   Forgiveness and Restitution
Sun. Luke vii, 36-50   The Love of the Forgiven

Hymnary 396: 'The King of Glory standeth'
     „   683: 'I will sing the wondrous story'

1. *Jesus as Saviour*

'Thou shalt call His name Jesus, for He shall save His people
from their sins' (Matt. i, 21). 'The Son of man is come to
seek and to save that which was lost' (Luke xix, 10). 'This is
My blood of the new testament, which is shed for many for
the remission of sins' (Matt. xxvi, 28). Sentences like these
focus to a point the truth which lies on every page of the
Gospels, that the coming of Christ was God's plan for the
mending of a broken earth. The world to which Jesus came
was a world sorely damaged and defaced. Wherever Jesus
looked, He saw traces of the working of one disastrous
power. Wherever He went, He encountered men, potential
sons of God, whose fellowship with their Father in heaven
that one power had destroyed. All along the line, the progress of humanity was being held up and thwarted and
thrown into confusion by the one stubborn enemy. The
enemy was sin. Here was the ubiquitous fact with which
Jesus, in seeking to establish the Kingdom, had to deal. His
work on earth was the restoring of the family relationship,
the fellowship of children with their Father, which sin had
interrupted and overthrown. Accordingly, our aim in the

83

present study must be a twofold one, first to find what Jesus had to say, by word and attitude, about sin, the disease; and then to watch His discovery and application of the remedy, namely forgiveness.

It is significant fact that Jesus seems to have spoken but rarely of 'sin' in the singular, and nearly always of 'sins' in the plural. His interest, that is to say, was not abstract but concrete, not speculative but practical. Questions of the origin of sin, for instance, were not His primary concern; and the modern discussions of the part played in sin by the factors of environment and inheritance find but little place in the Gospels. Broken lives were never treated by Jesus as 'cases': they were brothers to be helped, and the personal interest was supreme. It was no part of Jesus' purpose to elaborate a theory of sin which would explain where it had come from, or why God should continue to tolerate it in His universe. What He attempted and gloriously carried through was something far greater than that, far more practical—the restoring of lost sons to the home in God from which their sins had shut them out.

2. *What Our Sins Meant to Jesus*

The Gospels make it clear that sin, to Jesus, meant anything and everything that might put a barrier between a man and his God, or between a man and his neighbour. Now here Jesus' thought moved along two distinct lines.

On the one hand, *sin was the breaking of a law*. This, at first sight, might seem to be no more than the Jewish Rabbis taught; they, too, held that the law was the final standard of righteousness, and any violation of the law was sin. But in reality Jesus went much deeper than this. He was not thinking, as the Rabbis were, of any ceremonial righteousness: He was thinking of God's law written in the secret places of men's hearts. It was Jesus who first revealed the true *inwardness* of sin. This He illustrated in the Sermon on the Mount, when He showed (as against the Rabbis) that sins may be committed in thought and desire, no less than in action, and that there are sins of the mind and spirit, as well as sins of the flesh (Matt. v, 21 f, 27 f). Pharisaism, which always waxed hot and indignant against sins of this latter kind, branding them as disreputable and fatal, took but little notice of such 'respectable' sins as pride and selfishness and lack of love; but it was precisely these things, these inward, spiritual sins, that called forth Christ's sternest denunciations. Bad as the sins of the flesh were, these were worse. Indeed, so strenuously did Jesus emphasize the essential inwardness of sin that it would not be wrong to say that He regarded sin, not primarily as something that a man does, but as something a man *is*. 'Those things', He said, 'which proceed out of the mouth come forth from the heart. Out of the heart proceed evil thoughts, murders, thefts' (Matt. xv, 18 f). Deep in the secret heart of man God's eternal law stands written; and sin is the breaking of that law.

But it is more. *It is a blow at a loving heart.* We talk about breaking a law; but that, after all, is only relatively true. In one sense, you cannot break a law: you can only be broken by it. But you *can* break a heart; and that comes nearer the truth about sin as Jesus saw it. Sin is not hurting the moral order, for an impersonal order cannot suffer. Sin is hurting love, and love can suffer dreadfully. 'O Jerusalem, Jerusalem,' cried Jesus on the Mount of Olives, 'how often would I, and ye would not!' (Matt. xxiii, 37). The deepest shadow in the story of the prodigal is not the sufferings of the sinful son: it is the sorrow of the lonely father (Luke xv, 11 ff). Sin, according to Jesus, is something more than the *Shorter Catechism* has put into its definition, 'any want of conformity unto, or transgression of, the law of God'. It is something more than a blundering running of our heads against the inexorable laws of the universe. It is another nail hammered into love's cross, a clenched fist thrust up into the face of God. It is a blow struck at a loving heart.

Hence there was no minimizing of our sins with Jesus. He never treated them lightly. He never excused or condoned them. Some of His contemporaries thought He did. The name 'Friend of sinners', which is today His glory, was originally flung at Him as a stinging gibe by His critics: to them, His readiness to consort with sinners of all kinds seemed to argue a deficient estimate of sin, and even a flaw in His own character (Matt. xi. 19). But they were forgetting, or more probably for their own ends they were deliberately ignoring, the fact that while Jesus loved all broken lives, He hated passionately the evil things that had broken them. He never spoke, like Augustine, of 'splendid sins'. Milton's Satan has a touch of glamour about him: there was no glamour in sin as Christ saw it. The idea that because God is kind and benevolent and understanding it is unnecessary to take sin too seriously, and that everything is bound to come right in the end (as in Heine's words, 'Of course God will pardon me: that is His job') received no countenance from Jesus for a moment. On the contrary, we have not learned much from the Gospels if we have failed to realise that every unlovely action a man does, and every unclean thought he thinks, have Jesus Christ against them, a Christ who in His mercy has to be quite merciless to sin, whose eyes are 'as a flame of fire' (Rev. i, 14). There was no blurring of moral distinctions with Jesus. He spoke of men as 'lost' (Matt. xviii, 11; Luke xv, 4, 8, 24), and 'perishing' (Matt. xviii, 14; John iii, 16). In the end, He proved His implacable antagonism to sin by dying at its hands. The Cross is the measure of Jesus' view of the seriousness of sin.

3. Sin's Consequences

We turn next to what Jesus had to say about *the consequences of our sins*. He recognized, to begin with, that sins are often visited with *outward penalties*. The precise connexion between sin and suffering is one of religion's perennial problems, and Jesus elaborated no theory about it: but He warned His hearers that God always takes men at their word, and that they must be prepared to find their sins calling forth a divine reaction. We inhabit a world made by God; it is a moral universe, and its heart is set on righteousness; and therefore we punish ourselves by our sins, as Charles Kingsley expressed it, 'just as a wheel in a piece of machinery punishes itself when it gets out of gear'. To one sufferer whom He healed, Jesus said, 'Sin no more,' adding significantly, 'lest a worse thing come upon thee' (John v, 14).

But it is quite clear that in Jesus' mind any such outward penalties of human sins were dwarfed by their inward results. One such result was *the bad conscience*. 'Father,' cried the prodigal, 'I have sinned against heaven, and in thy sight, and am no more worthy to be called thy son' (Luke xv, 21). It was the bad conscience that suddenly made cowards of a whole clamorous crowd when Jesus suggested that anyone among them who had no sin should cast the first stone (John viii, 9); that sent Peter out into the night, weeping bitterly (Matt. xxvi, 75); that drove Judas to his death (Matt. xxvii, 4 f).

Again, Jesus said that our sins result in *an enslaved will*. In His own declared programme, the central thing was this— 'to preach deliverance to the captives' (Luke iv, 18). 'Whosoever committeth sin', He said, 'is the servant—the bondslave—of sin' (John viii, 34). He meant that wrong thoughts, once admitted to a man's heart, begin to beat a track for themselves there, to drive a thoroughfare right through his experience, and that, when that path has been made, foul shapes of sin can march up and down it at will, with none to say them nay. It was the same enslaving power of sin that Marcus Aurelius was thinking of when he said, 'Whatever the mental pictures you often make, to that colour your mind comes; the mind is dyed by its pictures.' The sinner awakes one day to discover that, try as he may, he cannot forsake his sin. It has the whip-hand of him now. His will is enslaved.

Closely related to this is another consequence of sin which Jesus encountered, *the hardened heart*. When Jesus stood before Herod at the last, not a word would He speak (Luke xxiii, 9. Contrast His attitude towards Pilate, John xix, 33 ff). That silence could only mean one thing, that the man's spiritual faculty, on the day when the Son of God confronted him, was atrophied. This is what Scripture means by the hardening of a man's heart. It is not that God predestines any soul to destruction. It is not that God shuts any man out into darkness. But a man may shut himself out. He may go on in sin until he loses the very power of recognizing goodness when he sees it. It is the Nemesis of sin that it impairs the judgement and blinds the vision and hardens the heart, until even the glory of God on the face of Jesus Christ may mean just nothing. As Whittier expressed it:

> For ever round the mercy-seat
>   The guiding lights of love shall burn,
> But what if, habit-bound, thy feet
>   Shall lack the will to turn?
>
> What if thine eye refuse to see,
>   Thine ear of Heaven's free welcome fail,
> And thou a willing captive be,
>   Thyself thy own dark jail?

But the consequence of sin of which Jesus chiefly thought was *the loss of fellowship with God* which it involves. Supreme among all the blessings of life stood communion with the heavenly Father: hence the overwhelming gravity of sin, which always disturbs such communion. There might be love at home for the prodigal still, and an abundant welcome waiting for him when he came; but nothing could alter the fact that the lad in the far country had lost, for the time at least, his father's fellowship (Luke xv, 13). It is the pure in heart who see God (Matt. v, 8); and sin, which smirches the purity, also spoils the vision. What mainly struck Jesus about the sinner's lot was its utter loneliness (Luke xv, 4); and the worst element in that loneliness was not the separation of the sinner from his brother men, though that, too, was involved. It was his isolation from God.

Jesus also pointed out that one man's sins inevitably entail *consequences to others*. 'Whatsoever a man soweth, that shall he also reap' (Gal. vi, 7) is not the whole truth, for others have to share the reaping. Others have to pay part of the price; and sometimes they pay in sorrow and suffering and tears, like the poor who are ruined by others' greed (Luke xx, 47), or like the father whose boy goes wrong (Luke xv, 11); and sometimes they even pay in sin, like God's 'little ones' to whom others play the tempter (Matt. xviii, 6). This is a

direct outcome of what we may call the 'solidarity' of life.
'Our echoes', says Tennyson, 'roll from soul to soul.' No
doubt the prodigal told himself that his way of life was his
own private affair, and that if there should be a price to pay
in the end for the far country's pleasures he would have had
his day and would be ready to pay up without whimpering;
but he was wrong. There were others who were going to
pay. Already his own father was paying. Shakespeare's
Richard cries:

> O God! if my deep prayers cannot appease Thee
> But Thou wilt be avenged on my misdeeds,
> Yet execute Thy wrath on me alone!

That cannot be. Sin's tragedy is that it always involves others.
And it was just the supreme instance of this when one day
it involved God Himself in a Cross.

The ultimate consequence of sin, according to Jesus, is
judgement. Attempts are continually being made to explain
away this element in Jesus' teaching, and to construct a
religion with the thought of judgement left out. Such
attempts will always be foredoomed to failure. The fact of
judgement is rooted firmly in passage after passage of the
Master's teaching (e.g. Matt. xxv; Luke xii); and a religion
in which this idea found no place could be constructed only
at the price of mutilating the Gospels beyond recognition.
Of course, we are not to interpret with a crude literalism
language which Jesus always meant to be taken pictorially;
but from everything He said on this great theme one fact
shines out clearly, that sin, if persisted in, has consequences
which reach beyond this present world of time, and that
every one of us at the last shall give account of himself to
God. (See *Christian Faith and Practice*, Craig, Milligan and
Baillie, pp. 77 ff).

4. *Sin's Remedy*

But Jesus came to earth, not only to diagnose a malady, but
also to prescribe and apply the remedy. We turn now from
the disease to its cure. The remedy was forgiveness, the

reconciling of sinners to God, the restoring of the lost relationship. This, of course, is something quite different from the remitting of sin's penalty, for a forgiven man may still have to bear the cost of his misdeeds. From the moment when Jesus said to the penitent thief, 'Today shalt thou be with Me in Paradise' (Luke xxiii, 43), the man's sin was blotted out: and yet the full penalty of death was exacted. Still it would be wrong to suppose that forgiveness does not react even upon these outward penalties. It does. It changes them by changing the pardoned man's whole attitude to them: sometimes they even become means of grace. But after all, the bearing of sin's continued consequences is a very small matter when it is set alongside the experience of being put right with God. And it is in this that forgiveness essentially consists.

What, then, did Jesus teach, by word and deed, on this great matter? In the first place, He emphasized *the glorious reality of forgiveness*. Some were slow to credit this. Things could never be the same again, they felt. Sin had cut them off too drastically. The old intimacy of fellowship could never come back. This lurking doubt was very poignantly expressed by Jesus in His greatest parable. When the lad who had smirched his honour and ruined his good name came limping back, a poor shabby wreck of the life that had set out from home so gaily and buoyantly not long before, he felt that he could never hope to be one of the family again —that would be too much to ask. 'I am no more worthy to be called thy son: make me as one of thy hired servants' (Luke xv, 19). Men felt like debtors confronting liabilities which it was utterly and for ever impossible for them to meet (Matt. xviii, 23 ff; Luke vii, 41 ff). Into that feeling of hopelessness Christ broke with the glorious news of full and final restoration. Before ever the prodigal could get out his suggestion about the 'hired servant', his father's arms were round him (Luke xv, 20). The creditor wiped the slate clean (Luke vii, 42). There was no long period of probation: in a single moment, a man might leap clear from the fearful pit to the very breast of eternal love, and the most wasted, shrivelled, burnt-out soul might stand erect and clean and in its right mind before God (Luke xxiii, 43).

Another fact which Jesus made very clear was that in restoring the lost relationship *God holds the initiative*. It is from God's side, not the sinner's side, that everything begins. Human efforts to earn and to achieve pardon are unavailing. We cannot, to use Robert Browning's words in *Johannes Agricola*,

> Make out, and reckon on, His ways,
> And bargain for His love, and stand,
> Paying a price, at His right hand.

The Parable of the Labourers in the Vineyard settled that once for all: in forgiveness, there is no question of merit, but all is of grace (Matt. xx, 1-16). Even penitence, without which pardoning love cannot become operative, is God-created, not man-made. It is God's goodness and love, especially as these are manifested in Jesus, which evoke the penitence. So it was with Peter after his denial. 'The Lord turned, and looked upon Peter. And Peter remembered' (Luke xxii, 61). Then penitence came like a flood. Always God holds the initiative. It is one of the secrets of the saving power of Calvary that the sight of the Cross can produce in a man's heart a sorrow and a shame for sin which he himself could never create. Everything in the experience of being forgiven, penitence included, is the gift of God.

Notice, further, *the central place of Jesus in forgiveness*. He not only declared forgiveness. He embodied it. Sinners encountering Jesus became aware of a double effect He had upon them. On the one hand, His sinless purity searched and scorched their souls. His holiness was like a mirror in which, for the first time in their lives, they really saw themselves as they were. It happened to Peter at the beginning of his discipleship. 'Depart from me, ' he cried, 'for I am a sinful man, O Lord' (Luke v, 8). It happened to the woman of Samaria. 'Come,' she exclaimed, 'see a man, which told me all things that ever I did' (John iv, 29). On the other hand, there was something in Jesus' presence that chased sinners' despair away and gave birth to a great hope. When Jesus walked down the road with despised Zacchaeus at His side, He was no doubt losing for Himself the respect of the crowd, but He was not thinking of that. He was restoring the man's long-vanished self-respect, and that was the first step in his salvation (Luke xix, 6, 7). Men felt, when they encountered Jesus, that here was One who believed in them, even when they had ceased to believe in themselves, One who was quite sure that they and He together could yet make something big and fine and clean of life: and with that, hope that had been dead came alive again, and the way for the miracle of forgiving love was open. Jesus, by His very attitude to them, made the fact of forgiveness credible; for they felt, dimly no doubt at first, but always with growing clearness, that the love which had followed them down to the depths and now stood by them in their shame was the love of God Himself.

The Gospels further make it clear that *Jesus connected the forgiveness of sins with His own death* (Matt. xx, 28; xxvi, 28). He knew, as we have already seen, that His death, by exposing sin in its true nature, would create penitence, and so make forgiveness possible (John xii, 32). But He also knew that the same Cross which thus uncovered the sin of man would reveal the very heart of God. Hence He was not driven to His death; it was His choice, and He went to it in the freedom of His soul. We shall have to return to the meaning of the death of Jesus at a later point in our study (see pp. 177 ff): suffice it here to say that sinners, looking at the Cross, have always seen in it, not Jesus' love only, but God's love, not merely the sacrifice of the Son, but the sacrifice of the Father. That is what makes the love of Calvary an overpowering thing, infinitely strong to save. 'God was in Christ, reconciling the world unto Himself' (2 Cor. v. 19).

Finally, Jesus spoke of *the results of forgiveness*. Two results He confidently looked for in the lives of the forgiven. He looked for love. And He was never disappointed: love always came. The breaking of the alabaster box, as Jesus Himself pointed out to Simon the Pharisee, was a symbol of the newborn love which the experience of a great pardon had created (Luke vii, 37 ff). And He looked for goodness. He expected forgiveness to be a regenerative force, re-making character. And here again His hopes were realized. Zacchaeus, having been saved, immediately and of his own accord faced up to the moral issues of salvation: he an-nounced his purpose of restitution (Luke xix, 8). What made Peter the mighty apostle that he became was the dis-covery that Jesus had forgiven him for the hour of black shame in the high priest's courtyard, and was willing, with the gracious words 'Feed My sheep', to trust him all over again; that made him a man of God indeed (John xxi, 15 ff). No one who reads the Gospels will ever be led astray by the argument that to pardon freely is simply to condone sin, and therefore to make for the demoralization of the sinner. To know oneself forgiven, and forgiven at so great a cost, is always a moral dynamic of the first order. It is a main-spring of the dedicated life. It creates character. It works righteousness. It brings honour back to the throne. It makes the forgiven sinner Christ's man, body and soul, for ever.

11: THE MINISTRY OF HEALING

Mon.	Matt. viii, 1-17	Typical Works of Mercy
Tues.	Mark i, 23-28	Devils Cast Out
Wed.	Mark i, 40-45	The Leper Cured
Thur.	Mark x, 46-52	Blind Bartimaeus
Fri.	John xi, 35-45	The Raising of Lazarus
Sat.	Matt. xvii, 14-21	The Necessity of Faith
Sun.	Luke xi, 14-23	
		The Defeat of the Kingdom of Evil

Hymnary 86: 'Thine arm, O Lord, in days of old'
    "   353: 'Father, whose will is life and good'

1. *The Good Physician*

There are two possible ways of approaching this subject. Either we can single out from the Gospel story one typical instance where Christ wrought a cure, and try to probe its methods and its meaning; or else we can take the Gospel picture as a whole, and let that speak to us of His healing work. Here we shall take the second way.

Let us begin with this. *The ministry of healing was an integral part of the work Christ came into the world to do.* It was an essential element of His mission and vocation. In no sense was it a side-issue. It was a function which Jesus Himself invariably ranked along with His teaching and preaching. The healing miracles were no mere incidental works of pity, but the fruit of Jesus' strong conviction that He had come into the world to redeem our human personality in all its aspects, physical as well as spiritual, and to offer unto God His Father whole men. And indeed we can see that, if He was to be Redeemer at all, He was bound to take that line. For soul and body are inextricably welded together, and are continually acting and reacting on each other. Hence the ministry of healing was an integral part of Christ's God-given task.

He recognized it as that Himself: for when he sent His followers out to carry on His work, it was with a dual commission that He sent them—to preach and to heal (Mark iii, 15; Luke x, 9).

Accordingly, any efforts which may be made to eliminate this side of things from the story, to draw Christ as the winsome Teacher and persuasive Preacher and nothing more, to construct a Gospel with these mighty works of healing, and indeed everything that is commonly ranked under the name 'miracle', left out—any such efforts are fore-doomed to failure. No doubt there will always be some people who declare that if these things were away a stumbling-block to faith would be removed. Some there may be who would almost prefer Jesus the simple Teacher. But one thing is certain—eliminate the supernatural from your thoughts of Jesus, and you may still have something that you find valuable left: you have certainly not the Christ of the Gospels left, but a different being altogether. Beyond all question, the mighty works of Jesus are part of the very texture of the evangelical record, and a main part of our Lord's mission to the earth.

2. *The Compassion of Christ*

The fact, then, of the healing ministry of Jesus is fixed and clear. What we have to do now is to try to interpret that fact. We have to explore its Why and its How. In other words, two questions confront us, one a question of Motive, the other a question of Method. Why did Jesus devote Himself to the curing of disease? And how were His cures wrought?

Take first the question of Motive. Now, according to one view, the answer to that question is simple: Jesus did His mighty works with the deliberate aim of drawing attention to Himself, proving His divinity, and so enforcing His teaching. It was necessary (so this view holds) for Jesus to draw attention to Himself, and these dramatic works were His chosen way of doing it. They were the trumpet Jesus sounded to attract the world's notice. They were the credentials Jesus offered the world in proof of His claims. They were the testimonials of the Master's divinity. Their motive was self-authentication. They were there to create belief in Christ.

It needs only a little thought to show how wide of the mark this view is. For one thing, it directly contradicts the evidence of the Gospels themselves. It says that Jesus did His mighty works in order to draw attention to Himself and broadcast His claims. Is that what the Gospels say? On the contrary, the Gospels give us a Christ who fled from fame. The Gospels give a Christ who again and again followed up His cures with an immediate injunction to secrecy. 'See thou tell no man!' (Matt. viii, 4; Mark viii, 26; Luke viii, 56). Does that look like broadcasting His claims? And why was Jesus so emphatic about secrecy, so determined *not* to make miracles a kind of public testimonial to Himself? Because the whole idea of appealing to men by miracles, the whole method of driving men into belief in Himself by startling, dramatic deeds, was foreign to His nature. Out in the desert of the Temptation, He renounced once for all the chance of getting on to the throne of the world by the miraculous. That is what His refusal of the suggestion to throw Himself down from the pinnacle of the Temple meant. If He was to win the hearts of men at all, it was to be not by startling miracle, but by simple holiness and suffering love. Whatever the motive of the healing ministry may have been, it was not to accredit Himself.

Moreover, there is this to be added. If Jesus' motive for His mighty works had been to prove His divinity, surely He would have kept the power of doing such works to Himself. But what we find in the Gospels is the very reverse. Jesus believed that men, ordinary men, could share that power. Indeed, He deliberately transmitted His own power to others. Quite certainly He meant His first disciples to exercise it too. And quite certainly they did, in some degree, exercise it. Hence His ruling motive cannot have been to raise Himself to lonely divine grandeur.

In any case, such a motive would have failed of its effect: miracles do not, and never will, create belief, not real saving belief at any rate. And Jesus knew that perfectly. 'If they hear not Moses and the prophets,' He said, 'neither will they be persuaded, though one rose from the dead' (Luke xvi, 31), a statement which was amply verified when Christ Himself rose from the dead. That is not how Christian conviction comes. To begin with miracles and argue from them up to Christ is beginning at the wrong end. And in point of fact, that is not how we became believers. It was not by accepting the miracles that we grew convinced of Christ. But it was because we had already grown convinced of Christ, along other lines, that we can accept the miracles—a very different thing. Let us keep our perspective right. The mighty works of Jesus must have had some other deeper motive than a mere demonstration and proof of power.

According to the Gospels, there were two motives. On the one hand, there was *Christ's compassion for all hurt things*. When Jesus laid His hands upon a leper's sores, it was not with an eye to effect, any more than His taking the children to His arms had an eye to the effect on the spectators. Any such idea of Jesus trying to produce a favourable impression is horrible. It would give us an unnatural Christ. No. Jesus carried the lambs in His bosom because He loved them— just that; and Jesus touched the leper's sores because He pitied him with all His heart. The ruling motive of the mighty works of Jesus was always and everywhere compassion.

And it was not a cheap compassion. The word 'compassion' is a compound of two Latin words, and means 'suffering with'. That is what it meant for Jesus—suffering with the leper, suffering with the epileptic, suffering with the anxious father, suffering with the broken-hearted mother. So absolute was His self-identification with His brothers and sisters of the earth that every wound of theirs was His wound too, every pain His pain, every sorrow His sorrow. Roman Catholics sometimes speak of 'the five wounds of Jesus', meaning the four nail-prints and the spear-thrust. Five wounds? The heart of Jesus carried a thousand wounds. 'Himself,' said Matthew, quoting Isaiah, for he had seen at close quarters what this redeeming compassion was costing his Master, 'Himself took our infirmities, and bare our sicknesses' (Matt. viii, 17; Isa. liii, 4). And often the compassion that healed was an agony.

The other motive of Christ's mighty works which the Gospels suggest is this: *in God's world Jesus always regarded disease as an intruder*. It was not part of the plan. It was not directly devised by God's goodwill. It was not native to God's Kingdom. It was alien. Therefore Jesus, whenever He met it, set Himself to destroy it.

This aspect of the matter has not been adequately emphasized. There was no false resignation about Jesus. Never was a sufferer turned away with the words, 'I am sorry, friend, but I cannot heal you, because God wants you to suffer.' Jesus was not resigned to leprosy. He was not resigned to the sobs of little children. Where this whole darker side of human life is concerned, Christ was never a model of acquiescence. Christ was first and last a fighter. No doubt in a sense it is a true philosophy which says, 'God's in His heaven, all's right with the world.' But it is a deeper, truer philosophy which says that Christ is God come out of His heaven because things were wrong with the world, God come forth to challenge the alien, intruding things, and to put a wrong world right.

In this connexion it is interesting to notice that Jesus often used the work of healing, both His own and His followers' work, to illustrate the break-up of the kingdom of Satan. Remember that in Jesus' day diseases were regularly attributed to demonic agency, not only cases of 'possession' (which were most obviously attributable to evil spirits) but all kinds of sickness. The unseen world was held to be full of these malign influences, emissaries of the Evil One. Hence, whenever a cure was wrought, it meant that one of these spirits had been cast out. And therefore when, through Jesus and His followers, the work of healing suddenly began to go forward on a gigantic scale, it meant that the whole kingdom of evil and darkness and Satan was being shaken to its foundations, was indeed breaking up, and the kingdom of goodness and light and God was at last coming into its own. 'If I with the finger of God cast out devils,' said Jesus, 'no doubt the kingdom of God is come upon you' (Luke xi, 20). And when His seventy followers came back with news of marvellous cures, Jesus rejoiced in spirit and cried, 'I beheld Satan as lightning fall from heaven' (Luke x, 18). Hence the miracles, which were primarily works of divine compassion, were also illustrations of the great central theme of the Master's teaching, that the Kingdom of God was at hand.

3. *The Power of God in Jesus*

Up to this point, we have been considering the question of Motive, the Why of Jesus' healing ministry. We turn now from the Why to the How, the question of Method. *How were His cures wrought?*

Right in the forefront of our answer one big fact must stand—*the sinlessness of Jesus, His moral perfection*. The mighty works of Jesus, it cannot be too strongly stressed, were in no sense a magical achievement: they were through and through a moral achievement.

We are apt to lay down the law as to what is possible, and what is not possible, in this world. But does not that, for beings like ourselves whose own nature has never quite escaped the thraldom and inevitable limitations that sin imposes, savour of unwarranted presumption? Suppose that one day there were to appear a being who, unlike ourselves, had escaped that thraldom and those limitations and was absolutely and finally pure and sinless, then obviously you would have a new, unprecedented, incalculable factor upon the scene; and who can tell but that that incalculable purity might also liberate incalculable energies?

> My strength is as the strength of ten,
> Because my heart is pure

sings the poet. If, as that implies, strength of personality varies in direct proportion to purity of life (and there is evidence enough to show that in a very real sense it does), then absolute purity might well be matched with absolute strength of saving personality.

Now the point is that that sinless Being has appeared. In Jesus of Nazareth, the unprecedented factor has arrived. Hence the mighty works of Jesus are not in any way surprising. The surprise would have been if He had not done them. They were the normal expression of His personality, the outflow of His moral uniqueness. And the supreme instance of this was the Resurrection. To the men of the early days who had felt at first-hand the impact of the sinless personality of Jesus, the Resurrection was never a problem. For they knew that in His moral perfection He was a conquering soul: therefore disease and death had to submit. (Note specially Acts ii, 24.) Let it be emphasized again—at the back of all Jesus' mighty works was that one unprecedented factor, a sinless personality. Perhaps if we were more like Jesus, the works that He did should we do also.

Alongside the sinlessness of Jesus stands another factor in His healing power—*His mighty faith in God*. 'Why could not we cast him out?' said the disciples to Jesus, when they had been trying to work a cure in a case of demon-possession and had lamentably failed. Straight as an arrow to its mark came the answer, 'Because of your unbelief' (Matt. xvii, 20). And Christ faced that same desperate case, and in a moment the cure had happened. They had tried to do it, half-doubting and wondering whether God's power could possibly get through here; and that half-doubt had blocked the channel completely, and God's power could not get through. Jesus had tried it, absolutely confident that God's power could get through here or anywhere; and that confidence had flung wide the gates and the power simply streamed through. 'Whatever ye shall ask, believing,' said Jesus, 'ye shall receive' (Matt. xxi, 22); and His own life was one long, stupendous application of that principle. The mighty works of Jesus were the Father's answers to the faith of the Son.

But more than Jesus' sinlessness and faith in God entered into the miracles. *Men's faith in Jesus, and through Jesus in God*, was also involved. There were times when Jesus found His passion to heal baulked, places where the Son of God's shadow fell and nothing happened: the sick were sick still, the maimed still maimed. Why? Because they were not expecting anything to happen. Nazareth was one of the places where that spirit thwarted love. 'Jesus?' they said incredulously, 'Why, He is one of ourselves—nothing to be looked for from Him!' In that atmosphere, says the Evangelist, Christ could not even begin to work (Matt. xiii, 58). Sometimes, too, where a rudimentary faith did exist, it was just a spark, and before anything could happen it had to be fanned into a flame. That was why Jesus sometimes spoke to His patient for a time before any healing word was given. That, too, is doubtless why He touched the maimed and wounded places (Mark vii, 33). It was to elicit faith, to crystallize the patient's vague hopes into real expectancy. Then the cure came—not before. What Jesus loved more than anything was to find a man who had daring enough to pitch his demands high and to be so sure that he was right to do it that he would simply take no denial (Mark x, 46 ff). Give Me faith like that, said Jesus, and all things will be possible!

But when all is said, the healing ministry of Jesus runs back to this, that *in Him the power of God was present in the earth*, and present in an absolutely unimpeded form at last. Everything turns on that. This was nothing less than the Spirit of God, the living God, in action. To the disciples, as they came to share something of that Spirit, something of the same power was given. But in the great words of the Fourth Gospel—'God gives Him the Spirit in no sparing measure' (John iii, 34, Moffatt). The story of Jesus, who went about continually doing good to men, is the story of immeasurable energy in contact with measurable need. Here the eternal love of heaven was meeting the transient tragedies of earth. Nothing else could have happened on that battlefield but what did happen: need and tragedy had to own themselves defeated, and love and life were victors. For the work of Jesus was the work of the everlasting God.

12: THE PRAYER LIFE OF JESUS

Psalm lxi, 1-5: 'O God, give ear unto my cry'
Hymnary 457: 'O for a closer walk with God'

1. *Teach Us to Pray*

A sentence of St. Luke's gives us our starting-point. 'It came to pass that, as He was praying in a certain place, when He ceased, one of His disciples said unto Him, Lord, teach us to pray' (Luke xi, 1). We are not to suppose, of course, that before this the disciples had never prayed, and that now they were just beginning. Probably all of them, or nearly all, were already men of prayer. Reared in devout and simple homes, Peter and Andrew and James and John had no doubt learnt to say their prayers at their mothers' knees. But note the particular circumstances of this request which St. Luke records. It was when Jesus had been praying with them, and the prayer was just finished, that the request was made. No doubt often before this they had felt the difference between Jesus' prayers and their own, His so sure and strong and real, theirs so weak and stammering and intermittent, His so comprehensive and God-inspired and prevailing, theirs so erratic and spasmodic and unsatisfying. But today that difference had come home to them with a rush of overwhelming awe, and they suddenly felt that if this was prayer they had still to learn the very rudiments of it. 'Lord,' they said beseechingly when that evening's worship was over, 'Lord, teach us to pray.'

Two preliminary points are worthy of notice. One is the striking fact that *Jesus never argued for the validity of prayer any more than He argued for the existence of God*. God was not something to be proved by argument: God was simply there, the beginning and the end of experience. Just so, prayer was not something to be proved by argument: prayer was there, the native breath of the soul. Prayer was man's instinctive tendency, wrought into the very constitution of his nature. Its well-springs lay deep down beneath the region of argument: they lay in hearts which God had made for fellowship with Himself, which therefore (as St. Augustine at a later day expressed it) would always be restless until they found their rest in Him. Hence Jesus never argued the matter. But certainly there was a sense in which His own prayer life was the one unanswerable argument. Did any disciple—Thomas for example—have doubts about prayer, genuine, honest doubts? Nothing was more likely to vanquish his doubts than the sight of Jesus upon His knees. For knowing Jesus, and realizing what an utterly sure and reliable insight Jesus had into all the deepest things of life, such a disciple would feel it better to trust Jesus' certainty rather than his own uncertainty. He would think it wise to attach more importance to Christ's conviction than to his own doubts. In all matters of faith this is an enormously valuable principle; and certainly it carries weight here. Doubts are dispelled and dissolved before the shining prayer life of the Christ. The praying Christ is the supreme argument for prayer.

The other preliminary point to be noticed is this, that when the disciples went to school with Jesus in this matter of prayer, there were really two departments in the curriculum, *the precepts of Jesus, and the practice of Jesus*. On the one hand, there were the things the Master said about prayer, His deliberate lessons on the subject; on the other hand, there was His own life of communion with God. Now it is not really possible to keep these two aspects separate. At every point they meet and mingle. Christ's teaching about prayer was the fruit of His own secret life of prayer: and His life of prayer was simply His teaching in action. Hence we shall draw upon them both equally and indiscriminately in our study here.

There are three great facts which claim our attention. *First*, prayer was the habitual atmosphere of Jesus' daily life. *Second*, Jesus was found praying at all the great crises of His career. *Third*, our Lord's prayers contained many different elements, petition as well as communion, intercession no less than thanksgiving.

2. *The Practice of the Presence of God*

Prayer was the habitual atmosphere of Jesus' daily life. Evidence of this can be found on almost every page of the Gospels. We see Jesus rising up in the early morning to pray while all the world was still asleep, 'a great while before day', says St. Mark (i, 35); Jesus, after a day of incessant toil that might well have worn His spirit out, keeping His watch with God all through the night (Mark vi, 46); Jesus, when the crowds surged round Him and broke in upon His privacy and clamoured greedily for His help, sending His heart and thoughts heavenward to clutch for a moment at His Father's hand (Mark vii, 34). It is there on page after page of the Gospels. And when to all that there is added this fact, that by far the largest part of Jesus' prayer life must have been secret, beyond the observation of the Twelve and even of Peter, James, and John, the most intimate three, and therefore unrecorded in any of the Gospels, we begin to realize that prayer was not only an important part of His life: it *was* His life, the very breath of His being.

This means that none of the things which commonly thwart and stifle our human prayers had any power at all with Christ.

Thus, for example, His prayer life was never at the mercy of *moods*. Changes of feeling Jesus certainly knew. He was no passionless Stoic. He knew joy and sorrow, smiles and tears, ecstasy and weariness. But through it all, His heart turned to prayer, like the compass to the north. Prayer meant communing with the One He loved best in heaven and earth. Jesus loved God His Father so utterly and so passionately

that He could not bear to be away from Him, but used every
opportunity the days and nights brought Him to go and
speak to the God of His love again. This means that those
failures in our own prayer life which we trace back to lack
of mood are really, according to Jesus, a symptom of something deeper; they are a symptom of a breakdown of affection.
Christ bids us go and give God our love.

Another thing which commonly stifles prayer is men's
busyness. The days become so full that prayer gets crowded
out. Sometimes when that happens the plea is urged in ex-
tenuation that work itself is prayer, that honest work is
indeed one of the highest kinds of prayer which can ever be
offered, and that, therefore, the crowding out of the devotional hour does not really matter very much. But look at
Jesus. Busy and crowded as our days are, His were emphatically more so. Read the opening chapters of St. Mark's
Gospel. There you have a number of pictures of typical days
in Jesus' ministry, days that were quite usual and normal
for Jesus; and as you study these pictures and see how one
duty was heaped upon another, how sick people and broken
sinners came clamouring for Him until far into the night
and none of them were sent away unhelped, you can almost
see the virtue going out of Him and can realize something
of the strain and the drain of it; and yet the harder the days
were, the more time did Jesus make for prayer. There was
a whole world to be redeemed, and He alone was to be
Redeemer. There was a thoroughgoing revolution in men's
thinking and men's morals to be achieved, and He had only
His own body and soul as instruments of that revolution.
Yet the world's greatest toiler was also the world's most
shining example of the daily, hourly practice of the presence
of God. And as for the plea, true no doubt up to a point,
that work itself is prayer, never for a moment would Jesus
countenance it when it made work a substitute for prayer.
The whole force of Christ's precept and practice was this,
that there could be *no* substitute for prayer. However busy
a man's life, he must, he can, make time to shut the door
and kneel.

Still another thing which often thwarts prayer is men's *impatience*. They think the door ought to open at their first knock; and when it does not open, they give up knocking and turn away. How different it was with Jesus! The writer to the Hebrews in one place speaks of Jesus offering up 'prayers and supplications, with strong crying and tears, unto Him that was able to save Him' (v, 7); and whatever else that may mean, it certainly means this, that prayer for Jesus was a strenuous, serious business, involving every energy of mind and heart and soul. It is the same truth that shines out of the great parable of the man who knocked at his neighbour's door at midnight (Luke xi, 5 ff). 'Shameless' (verse 8), Jesus calls him, and then blesses him for his shamelessness! 'That is the very spirit of prayer,' He says in effect. 'Take no denial! Knock again! Beat at heaven's gate!' Of course Jesus never meant to imply that God was unwilling to give or churlish to His children's cry; but He did mean that lackadaisical, half-hearted praying was worse than useless, and that often it is only when a man's importunity has given proof of his earnestness that the answer of God can come. That was the reason why Jesus always had a special love for people who came to Him and would simply take no denial—the Syrophoenician woman who refused to go away (Mark vii, 25 ff), blind Bartimaeus at the roadside, whose 'Son of David, have mercy' no threats or entreaties could silence (Mark x, 46 ff), the men who, finding the door blocked, broke up the roof rather than go away disappointed (Mark ii, 4 ff). If Jesus had a special love for these, it was because He felt that here was the very spirit that would prevail with God; here was real prayer in action. So men's impatience in prayer stands rebuked.

Finally, there are *moral difficulties* that sometimes impede our human prayers. Communion with God inevitably grows feeble and unreal if in our own lives there is some moral decision which we are not prepared to face. A background of absolute moral honesty is the first essential of prayer. Only the pure in heart, said Jesus, can see God. Electricians speak of certain substances as 'insulators', meaning that these automatically break the contact and cut off the current. Sin is an insulator that breaks our prayer contact with God. 'If I regard iniquity in my heart,' said the Psalmist, 'the Lord will not hear me' (Ps. lxvi, 18). This is the root of most of our troubles with prayer. But clearly this never laid an inhibiting hand upon the prayers of Jesus. Tempted in all points like ourselves, He kept His soul free from the faintest shadow of sin. Purity of heart sees God, and Christ's matchless purity saw God continually. Nothing was allowed to break the contact of the Son with the Father.

We see, then, that the things which commonly thwart and stifle our human prayers had no power with Christ. Prayer was the habitual atmosphere of His daily life. That is our first great fact. We turn now to the second.

3. Prayer and Crisis

Jesus was found praying at all the great crises of His career. There was a day when His call came, a sudden, swift summons to His life-work. 'It came to pass', says St. Luke, 'that Jesus being baptized, and praying, the heaven was opened, and the Holy Ghost descended' (Luke iii, 21). There you have Jesus praying *about His vocation.* There was a day when the first apostolic band had to be chosen, and the momentous decision made about the right men for carrying on His work. St. Luke, describing the night before the decision, says, 'He went out into a mountain to pray, and continued all night in prayer to God' (Luke vi, 12). There you have Jesus praying *for guidance.* There was a day when all the Twelve had been baffled by a peculiarly difficult case of demon-possession which seemed quite incurable, and only when they had given it up as hopeless and referred it to Jesus was healing wrought and the evil spirit cast out. 'Why could not we cast him out?' they asked Jesus later. And the answer was—'This kind can come forth by nothing but by prayer' (Mark ix, 29). There you have Jesus praying *for strength for His mighty works.* There was a day when Gethsemane closed round Him, and the hour and power of darkness had come, and the temptation to desert God's high road grew fierce. 'Being in an agony,' says the Evangelist, 'He prayed' (Luke xxii, 44). There you have Jesus praying *against temptation*. And finally there was an hour when the nails and torture of Calvary had almost finished their work, and strength was ebbing all away, and Jordan rolled its waters at His feet. 'Father,' cried Jesus, 'into Thy hands I commend My spirit' (Luke xxiii, 46). There you have the Jesus who *died praying*. So at all the great crises of His career, and even in the moment of death, Christ was found in prayer.

Now there, too, He was a pattern to His first followers, and to all other followers for ever. For crises such as these through which Christ prayed His way come to all the sons of men. The true disciple, like his Master, will be found praying at the opening of his life-work, praying for guidance in all life's momentous decisions, praying for strength to do the works of God, praying for victory when temptation assaults, praying when on his day of life the night is falling. Every hour of crisis will find him, as it found Jesus, deep in prayer.

4. *Factors in Prayer*

We turn finally to the third great fact which emerges from the Gospel picture of the prayer life of Jesus: *the prayers of our Lord had many different elements in them, communion, thanksgiving, petition, intercession.*

Communion—for often Jesus would turn to God, not for the sake of any gift that He was needing, but simply for the sake of God's own fellowship. 'As He prayed,' says St. Luke, describing one such occasion, 'the fashion of His countenance was altered' (Luke ix, 29). That was the prayer of communion, when heart spoke to heart, the Spirit of Jesus on the mountain to the Spirit of His Father in heaven; and so deep and rich and precious was that hour of utter intimacy that Jesus, as the Evangelist says, came out of it with the glow and wonder of it written on His very face, making it radiant like an angel's. The prayer life of Jesus warns us against the view that would make prayer a mere asking things from God. We do not make our human friendships mere matters of convenience, approaching our friend only when we desire a favour from him, and never going near him at any other time. No friendship could survive long on these mercenary terms. And Jesus would have us reflect that least of all can our friendship with God survive on such a basis. Jesus would have men go to God when there is nothing to ask, go to Him not for His gifts but for Himself alone. That is the prayer of communion, and when a human heart goes out Godward in this way, God comes to meet it, and it experiences the blessed invasion of God's presence. In such an experience a man's whole life, like the face of the Christ who prayed on the Mount of Transfiguration, is changed, for it comes to bear something of the afterglow of heaven.

Thanksgiving was another element of which Christ's prayers were full. It was often praise and gratitude that drove Him to His knees. Never did there creep into His prayers that note of aggrieved, protesting querulousness which sometimes marks our own. Always it was the amazing goodness of God His Father that filled and flooded His soul. And it was not only life's sunshine splendours that brought the cry of thanksgiving to His lips: the darkness found His gratitude unquenched. He took the broken bread, symbol of His broken body, and gave God thanks (Luke xxii, 19). He took the cup, seeing His own blood in it, and gave God thanks (Luke xxii, 17). He went out from the upper room to the sweat and agony of Gethsemane, singing a hymn, and giving God thanks (Mark xiv, 26). In the darkness as in the light, praise was the dominant note of Jesus' prayers; and not the Cross itself could silence it.

Another element in Jesus' prayers was *Petition*. We have seen already that asking for God's gifts was certainly not the whole or even the main part of the Master's prayer life; but we must be careful not to go to the other extreme and imagine that such petitionary prayers found no place at all. It is particularly necessary at the present time to emphasize this, for there is a dangerous tendency today, even among good Christian people, to speak disparagingly of petitionary prayers, and to say that asking for definite things from God is prayer of such a rudimentary and childish form that it ought to have no place in the religion of the mature and fully developed believer. This we must quite definitely deny. The idea that it is expedient to outgrow petitionary prayer goes to pieces on one clear fact—Jesus never outgrew it. On the contrary, Jesus deliberately encouraged it and urged men to use it. He settled that once for all in the first two words of the great prayer He taught His disciples, 'When ye pray, say, Our Father' (Luke xi, 2). For if God is really your Father, and if you are really His child, it cannot be wrong to bring Him definite requests and petitions: indeed, it would be unnatural not to bring them. Such petitions, of course, must always be subject, in our case as in Christ's, to the great ruling condition—'Thy will be done' (Matt. xxvi, 39); for God's wisdom may have to refuse what our heart craves. But our point just now is this, that the tendency to disparage petitionary prayer argues chiefly a lack of faith. Down at its roots there is lurking the thought that God is not fully at liberty, but in some sense bound, in some degree a prisoner in His universe. And what Christ would have us realize is that God is alive and God is free, and that therefore true faith will always do as Jesus Himself did, and carry its requests straight to the throne.

Finally, Jesus' prayers contained much *Intercession*. He prayed for the little children (Mark x, 16). He prayed on the Cross for His enemies (Luke xxiii, 24). He prayed for His disciples (John xvii, 9). He prayed for Judas. How terribly He wrestled in prayer for the soul of Judas only God and Jesus knew. One day when alone with His disciples, He exclaimed, 'Simon, Simon, behold Satan hath desired to have you, that he may sift you as wheat: but I have prayed for thee, that thy faith fail not' (Luke xxii, 31 f); and we cannot but feel that it must have meant something mighty to Peter to know that the everlasting arms of that intercession were underneath him, bearing him up.

Then though our foul and limitless transgression
  Grows with our growing, with our breath began,

Raise Thou the arms of endless intercession,
Jesus, divinest when Thou most art man!

And to every disciple that same priestly ministry of intercession has, under Jesus, been committed.

The practical conclusion to which our study of the prayer life of Jesus as revealed in the Gospels leads is that prayer must ever be the heart and centre of all true religion, and the dynamic and driving power of all the best and noblest living. When Bunyan's pilgrims were passing through the Enchanted Ground, they saw 'a man upon his knees, with hands and eyes lifted up, and speaking, as they thought, earnestly to one that was above. They drew nigh, but could not tell what he said; so they went softly till he had done. When he had done he got up, and began to run towards the Celestial City.' It is those who are often, like Mr Standfast, upon their knees, speaking earnestly to One above, who are able to march and run where others only halt and stumble. It is those who have learned the way of prayer from Jesus who have found the secret of victorious life. They go from strength to strength; every one of them appeareth before God in Zion.

13: THE GREAT CONFESSION

Mon.	Isa. xi, 1-10	The Hope of the Messiah
Tues.	Isa. liii	The Suffering Servant
Wed.	Matt. xi, 1-6	He that should come
Thur.	John vi, 59-69	To Whom shall we go?
Fri.	Matt. xvi, 13-21	At Caesarea Philippi
Sat.	John x, 22-38	The Son of God
Sun.	John v, 17-27	The Judge of Men

Psalm lxxii, 17-19: 'His name for ever shall endure'
Hymnary 507: 'I'm not ashamed to own my Lord'

1. *The Turning-point*

The day at Caesarea Philippi marks the watershed of the
Gospels. From this point onwards, the streams begin to
flow in another direction. The current of popularity which
seemed likely in the earlier days of Jesus' ministry to carry
Him to a throne has now been left behind. The tide sets
towards the Cross. The Galilean sunshine is suddenly
clouded over, and the air grows sultry and heavy with the
gathering storm. The voices shouting applause die away,
and another more ominous note is heard. At Caesarea Jesus
stood, as it were, on a dividing-line. It was like a hilltop
from which He could see behind Him all the road He had
travelled, and in front of Him the dark, forbidding way
awaiting Him. One look He cast back to where the afterglow of happy days still lingered, and then faced round and
marched forward towards the shadows. His course was now
set to Calvary.

Caesarea Philippi lay in the far north where the springs
of Jordan took their rise near the base of Mount Hermon.
Alone with His disciples in this remote, secluded region,
Jesus brought them face to face at last with the most momen-
tous question of their lives—'Whom say ye that I am?'
(Matt. xvi, 13 ff; Mark viii, 27 ff; Luke ix, 18 ff).

2. The Reserve of the Messiah

Now here it is necessary to remind ourselves that, whatever views and verdicts the disciples or the outside world may have formed about the position and personality of Jesus, His own mind, from the very opening of His ministry, was never visited by any shadow of doubt. He knew Himself to be Messiah. And (this goes even deeper) He knew Himself to be, in a unique and lonely sense, Son of God. It was that knowledge, as we have seen, which lay behind His three great original temptations: apart from it, the wilderness scene would be quite inexplicable. Certainly it was present at His baptism in Jordan. It is sometimes suggested that it was at the baptism that the awareness of Messiahship and Sonship first dawned on Jesus' soul; but surely it is far more probable that all through the silent Nazareth years the conviction was gradually taking shape, and that what happened in the hour of baptism was not a sudden awakening of Jesus to His own nature and function, but the receiving of power from on high, the setting of a seal by God upon the gradual discovery of years. In any case, it is clear that there never was a time in Jesus' ministry when He did not know Himself with utter certainty to be Messiah and Son of God.

But until this day at Caesarea that knowledge had been largely veiled. A certain reserve and reticence had characterized it. Jesus, knowing Himself Messiah, did not proclaim it from the housetops. The sick persons whom He healed were forbidden to publish the matter (Matt. viii, 4; ix, 30; Mark v, 43). The evil spirits who, feeling His power, guessed at His identity and shouted it aloud were condemned to silence (Mark i, 24). When John the Baptist from his prison put the question directly, 'Art Thou He that should come?' Jesus pointed away from Himself to His works, adding significantly, 'Blessed is he, whosoever shall not be offended in Me,' an answer which, while sufficiently revealing the truth to John, would not disclose it to others (Matt. xi, 2 ff). With the same end in view, He deliberately chose as His favourite title the enigmatic 'Son of Man'. This name had associations (notably Dan. vii, 13) which to the

spiritually-minded, and to them alone, would give a hint of
Jesus' Messianic dignity: to others it would convey nothing.
Only those who had 'ears to hear' would understand. Even
on the day of Caesarea Philippi itself, when the truth stood
fully revealed, Jesus 'charged His disciples that they should
tell no man that He was the Christ' (Matt. xvi, 20). As one
of our Scripture paraphrases puts it—

> His greatness He for us abased,
>   For us His glory veiled;
> In human likeness dwelt on earth,
>   His majesty concealed.

Why did Jesus practise this reserve? Not because His own
mind was troubled with doubts: that answer, as we have
just seen, is ruled out. There seem to have been two reasons.

On the one hand, the Messiah of whom the Jews for centuries had been dreaming was a very different being from
the Messiah whom God was now sending to them. The
popular expectation was full of political and nationalist
elements. The Messiah, when He came, would lift His
nation from the dust. He would forcibly restore the throne
of David. He would break the heathen with a rod of iron.
These were the hopes smouldering in men's hearts, and it
needed only the appearance of a Messianic claimant to fan
the glowing embers to a flame. It had happened in the past
when false Messiahs had arisen, and it would assuredly have
happened again if Jesus had chosen to press His claims from
the outset. The danger that the people 'would come and
take Him by force, to make Him a King' (John vi, 15)—a
King, that is, after their own national and mundane desires—
was never far away. Hence before Jesus could publicly proclaim Himself Messiah, He had to transform and spiritualize
the whole conception. He had to set it free from the political
accretions of centuries. In particular, He had to find a place
in it for the fact of suffering; the idea of a suffering Messiah
was utterly foreign to His contemporaries' thoughts. Here,
then, we have one reason for Jesus' reserve. His first aim,
He saw, must be to arouse men spiritually; till that was

done, the proclamation of Messiahship could only create misconception, and stimulate earthly, passionate hopes of a kind with which He was totally out of sympathy, hopes which, therefore, could never be fulfilled.

The other reason for Jesus' reticence (and this concerns His Sonship even more than His Messiahship) lay in the fact that the greatest truths can be revealed, not by words and proclamations, but only by life and love. One day when Jesus was walking in Solomon's porch in the Temple, a group of His fellow-countrymen accosted Him. 'How long dost Thou make us to doubt?' they said. 'If Thou be the Christ, tell us plainly' (John x, 24). But the greatest things in life cannot be 'told' in that way. Can you 'tell plainly' what honour is, or beauty, or love? Can you put a sunset into a sentence? Can you express the glory and mystery and magic of a great symphony in one terse phrase? None of life's really great, moving experiences or discoveries can be told plainly in words. And how should we expect the greatest and most moving of all to be thus told—which is the glory of God on the face of Jesus Christ? Jesus knew that it would not be by any voice proclaiming 'I am the Son of God' that conviction would be born in human hearts. But the wind bloweth where it listeth; and the men who live with Him and love Him learn His nature and His name.

3. The Greatest Question in the World

On that day at Caesarea Philippi, when the crowds had been left behind and He was alone with the Twelve, Jesus felt that all need for reserve was gone. Quite suddenly He put to them the most momentous question with which any soul can ever be faced, 'Whom say ye that I am?'

How all-important this question is, and how deep its practical issues for life, may be illustrated by the familiar story of Thomas Carlyle. On a day when death had darkened his home and his heart was sore, someone read to him the great words, 'Let not your heart be troubled. In My Father's house are many mansions' (John xiv, 1 ff). 'Aye,' broke out the bereaved man, 'if you were God, you had a right to say that; but if you were only a man, what do you know any more than the rest of us?' Always till then he had been inclined to regard the question about the divine-human nature of Jesus as a vague, remote, unpractical thing; but now suddenly, under the pressure of life, he had found that it mattered all the world to him, and that everything—hope, peace of mind, comfort—was bound up for him with the question of the nature and the rights of Jesus. It is the most momentous of all questions—'Whom say ye that I am?'

The Gospels make it quite clear why Jesus chose this particular juncture for His question. His reason was that He had something confidential to tell His disciples about the future, a disclosure to make which was bound to test and try their faith to the utmost, but which could now no longer be kept back from them. *He was going to tell them that He saw death coming to Him,* coming speedily, and coming with fearful shame (Matt. xvi, 21; Mark viii, 31; Luke ix, 22). And He may well have wondered—would that disclosure end their loyalty? Would they turn their backs on Him as so many others had done, and all His work be wasted? Everything depended on how high their faith in Him had risen. If that faith were weak, if it were still a halting, dim, uncertain thing, the shock of the news He had for them would certainly finish it. Clearly for Jesus, no less than for His disciples, it was an hour of crisis.

He began with the impersonal question—'Whom do men say that I am?' That, at any rate, was not difficult to answer. For on every side men were saying things about Jesus. A dozen verdicts were abroad. All kinds of rumours and opinions were in the air. Jesus was on every tongue. And men were not only saying things about Jesus; they were saying *great* things about Him. Some thought He was John the Baptist back from the dead. Others said He reminded them of Elijah. Others spoke of Jeremiah, or another of the prophets. In other words, while current opinions were by no means unanimous as to Jesus' identity, they were unanimous that He was someone great. His place was among the heroes of His race.

It is worth remarking that history is here repeating itself. Once again Jesus is on every tongue. He is being discussed today far beyond the circle of the Christian Church. And great is the diversity of verdicts about Him. Papini, looking at Jesus, sees the Poet. Bruce Barton sees the Man of Action. Middleton Murry sees the Mystic. Men with no brief for orthodoxy are ready to extol Jesus as the paragon of saints and captain of all moral leaders for ever. 'Even now', said John Stuart Mill, 'it would not be easy even for an unbeliever to find a better translation of the rule of virtue from the abstract into the concrete than to endeavour so to live that Christ would approve our life.' Like the men of His own day who called Him John, Elijah, Jeremiah, so the men of today are agreed that among the heroes and saints of all time Jesus stands supreme.

But Jesus was not content with that recognition. People were saying that He was John, Elijah, Jeremiah. But that meant that He was one in a series. It meant that there were precedents and parallels, and that even if He stood first in rank, He was still only *primus inter pares*, first amongst His equals. But quite certainly that is not what the Christ of the New Testament claimed. Men may agree with Christ's claim, or they may dissent from it; but as to the fact of the claim itself there is not the shadow of a doubt. Christ claimed to be something and Someone unprecedented, unparalleled, unrivalled, unique (e.g. Matt. xi, 27; x, 37; xxiv, 35; John x, 30; xiv, 6). No doubt the Roman Emperor who had a statue of Jesus and a statue of Plato side by side in his pantheon thought that he was paying the Master a noble tribute: and indeed, in a sense, he was: only that was not the Gospel. No doubt Ernest Renan, when he wrote of Jesus that 'He stood in the first rank of the grand family of the true sons of God', felt that he was according the Man of Nazareth royal honour and dignity; but again, it was not the Gospel. John the Baptist, Elijah, Jeremiah, Jesus—was that the final truth about the world's Redeemer? One in a list? Plato, Socrates Buddha, Jesus—is that the truth? St. Francis, St. Bernard, St. Augustine, Jesus—is that the truth? Men have been con-

E

tent with that answer sometimes: it has never contented
Jesus. And so here at Caesarea the 'Whom say men that I
am?' was left behind; and straight, swift, direct came this—
'Whom say *ye* that I am?'

Observe how Christ pushed beyond the impersonal discussion to the personal challenge. That was regularly His
way. You can see it in His conversation with the woman at
the well—first the general talk, then suddenly the rapier-
thrust at her own heart. You can see it in His interview with
Pontius Pilate, when the latter was questioning Him about
His kingly claims. Suddenly like an arrow came the challenge,
'Sayest thou this thing of thyself, or did others tell it thee
of Me?' Is this your own verdict, Pilate, or just rumour that
you are retailing at second-hand? Always, sooner or later,
Jesus brought things back to the personal issue. He was not
anxious for any second-hand opinions or verdicts by proxy.
What He wanted was the straight answer of a man's own
experience. Whom say *ye* that I am?

It ought here to be said that this question of Jesus is
being forced upon the world today from three sides. *History*
forces it upon us. This Jesus who 'doth bestride the narrow
world like a Colossus' in a far truer sense than Julius Caesar
ever did, or Alexander, or Napoleon; whose cause has died
a score of deaths down the centuries, only to come alive
again each time, more glorious than ever—who can He be?
The Bible forces it upon us. This carpenter's apprentice who
could make claims like 'All things are delivered unto Me
of My Father' (Matt. xi, 27); this wandering preacher who
could bid the whole labouring, heavy-laden world come to
Him for rest (verse 28)—who can He be? *Conscience* forces it
upon us. This Man whose words still stab us like the sword
of God, whose eyes still haunt us, whose pure, holy image
puts us on our honour to live clean—who can He be? The
world has no chance of escaping the question. And everything in religion and in life depends upon the answer.

4. *The Answer of Faith*

Simon Peter rose to it. He rose to it with all the daring of his impetuous, loving heart. Try to feel the tense drama of the moment. Here was this question which had never been asked before. Here was the question to which through long, patient months of personal training and fellowship Jesus had been leading His men up. He knew that upon the way in which they might answer it everything for the future of His work depended. And now it was asked. We may well believe that there was silence for a moment, for these twelve men were facing now the ultimate mystery of things and the unfathomable depths of the being of God. But suddenly Peter rose to it, rose above all the poor, levelling, half-believing answers of men, and rang out his own startling, tremendous answer—'Thou art the Christ, the Son of the living God!'

The question has sometimes been raised as to how much this confession of Peter's implied. Quite certainly it implied a recognition of Jesus as the long-looked-for Messiah of Israel. Others were ready to hail Jesus as one of the Messiah's heralds. That is what was meant by calling Him Elijah and Jeremiah; for the belief was that these great figures of the past were to reappear upon the earth before the Messianic age broke in. But Peter had caught the truth in a flash. This was no herald. This was the Christ of God Himself.

But does the confession of Jesus as Messiah have any relevance today? Was Messiahship not simply an old Jewish idea which has long ceased to be valid? To these questions we must reply that if the word and the conception were Jewish and local and temporal, as they undoubtedly were, the thing itself was universal and eternal. For what did the Messianic idea mean but just this—that Someone was coming who would be the hope of the world, the fulfilment of every promise, and the answer to every prayer, One who would straighten out all human tangles, and right all earthly wrongs and bring in a better day of God? That was the idea. And we can see that, so far from having lost its meaning by the passing of the years, it has now more meaning than ever. For we are being driven by the very stress of our difficulties to realise that the one hope of the world is the recognition

and the acceptance of Jesus as God's guiding word to our
generation. Everything depends upon whether we are ready
to say with Peter, 'Thou art the Christ.'

5. *The Divinity of Christ*

But did Peter mean more than this? 'Son of the living God',
he said. Now that would not necessarily mean anything
more than Messiah, for we know that in Jewish thought
and speech 'Son of God' and 'Messiah' were sometimes
synonymous terms. But surely on Peter's lips it did mean
something more. Through all these months, something had
been happening in the lives of Peter and his fellow-disciples,
which none of them until now had dared to put into words:
they were beginning to feel towards Jesus just as they had
always felt towards God. They found now that, when they
tried to think of God, it was Jesus' face they saw; and they
were glad to make to this Master of theirs that surrender of
life which only the God of heaven can legitimately claim
from any man. All that went into Peter's cry, 'Thou art the
Christ, the Son of the living God.'

There, then, was the great conviction. And we can see
now the line along which Peter had reached it. It was the
line along which this conviction must still come, if it is to
come at all. He came to it *by living in the company of Jesus*.
The conviction had not been there to begin with. When
Jesus went to Simon the fisherman and said, 'Follow Me,'
and when the man rose and followed, he did not fully realize
who it was he was following. His only thought then had
been, 'Here is the kind of Leader I have been looking for,
and I am going with Him now.' A very rudimentary faith!
Yes, but enough for a beginning. Indeed, it is not possible
to expect any more—for a beginning. Jesus never asked any
more. He never began by dictating to men what they were
to think of Him. He never put them through a catechism
about His divine claims. The great thing was that men
could begin with Jesus anywhere, just where they were.
Jesus accepted Peter gladly on these terms, not demanding
full belief at once, but waiting for belief to grow and mature.

And grow and mature it did. It was the long days and nights in Jesus' company, mounting into months and years, which ultimately made the man a believer. For every day he was hearing Jesus speak with a strange, incredible authority he had never heard in any voice before. Every day he was watching Jesus at work, and observing with growing admiration and wonder how more than equal He was to all emergencies. Every day he was seeing Jesus in contact with shattered, futile lives, and these lives going back to the world again changed in a way in which he had always thought it was absolutely impossible for anyone but God to change them. There was more even than that. In his own heart Peter knew that none but God could forgive sin: yet in his own heart there was a voice telling him with utter certainty that this Jesus had forgiven him, and had indeed done more than that, for He was now breaking the power of sin in His servant's life—a work which only the God of heaven could do. That is how Peter found who Christ was. When all is said, how else can anyone find it? This Jesus does for me what only God can do. This Jesus redeems my life as only the Eternal could redeem it. This Jesus floods my being as only the Father of heaven could flood it. What can I do but confess it? This is divine! 'Thou art the Christ, the Son of the living God.'

In the last resort, however, Peter's knowledge of the Messiahship and divinity of Christ came as an inward revelation from God. 'Flesh and blood hath not revealed it unto thee, but My Father which is in heaven.' It was not a discovery which the disciple by himself had achieved; and while Peter's quest for the truth had certainly opened up the way for the coming of the vision, yet the vision when it came was God's gift. It was God who had flashed it in upon him. The conviction was not man-made, but God-given. It had come upon Peter with inherent, compelling power, authenticating itself to his heart, so that, apart from any argument, independently of any logical proof or demonstration, the man could say with absolute assurance, 'I know.' Somewhere in Peter's heart God's bell had tolled, and in that moment he knew that in Jesus Christ he was touching the Eternal. Such moments of revelation are the very life of religion. Only God can make us finally sure of God.

6. The Rock

Very significant is the great burst of glowing emotion with which Jesus received His disciple's confession. 'Blessed art thou, Simon Bar-jona!' Here, felt Jesus, was ample reward for all the patience of the years. Here was something at last to show for the travail of His soul. Here was the assurance that, whatever might happen now, defeat, death, apparent disaster, the cause was safe. And with that, Jesus' heart was lifted up in a great exulting gratitude to God. It is a striking illustration of what one man's faith can mean to our Lord. 'Blessed art thou, Simon. Thou art Peter—a Rock; and upon this rock I will build My church.' It has been debated what Jesus was referring to by the 'rock'. Was it Peter the man? Or was it Peter's confession of faith? Surely it was both. It was on Peter as a believing man, on Peter as a fully surrendered man, that the Church was to be built. But clearly the promise goes far out beyond Peter and the first generation of Christians. It is on believing men, on surrendered men, down all the years that Christ has done His building, and it is on them He is building now. Are we the kind of material that Christ can build with? What is our faith and loyalty—drifting, shifting sand, or firm, resolute rock? These are questions which every Christian must face alone with his own soul and with God.

14: THE ROYAL LAW OF LOVE

1. A Royal Law

It is a royal law *because it is the law of a King*. 'Ye have heard that it hath been said, Thou shalt . . . hate thine enemy. But I say unto you,' (listen to the kingly authority of Jesus!) 'Love your enemies' (Matt. v, 43 f).

It is a royal law *because it takes precedence of every other law*. If we fail here, says Jesus, we fail all along the line. No imposing array of splendid virtues, no deep piety nor long prayers, have any weight at all with God if the spirit of love is lacking (Matt. v, 23 f). This is God's ultimate test of the reality of our religion. 'If a man has not the love of God shed abroad in his heart,' cried D. L. Moody, 'he has never been regenerated.' 'He that loveth not knoweth not God; for God is love' (1 John iv, 8).

It is a royal law *because to obey it makes life royally happy*. 'With what measure ye mete', said Jesus, 'it shall be measured to you again' (Matt. vii, 2). That means that an uncharitable attitude is a boomerang: it comes back on the man who uses it. But it means also that as surely as an unloving spirit towards others poisons in the long run the atmosphere of a man's own life, so surely does a loving spirit sweeten it. Every man comes ultimately to inhabit the kind of world he makes for himself; and it is only the man who lives by love who can taste the gladness of God.

2. Love's Meaning

What kind of love was it that Jesus commended and extolled? Certainly not a genial amiability and good nature with no moral backbone, no power of standing up to the biting east winds of truth. Certainly not an all-inclusive toleration which allows the eternal distinctions of right and wrong to be blurred. The Christ who could speak the terrible words about the millstone and the depths of the sea (Matt. xviii, 6), the Christ of the whip of cords (Matt. xxi, 12; John ii, 15), never counselled an easy-going benevolence indifferent to moral values. That is not Christian love: that is unchristian laziness. What Jesus did mean by love was a spirit that never harbours a grudge, because it is much too big for that kind of pettiness; that always discovers the best in men, because it can see underground; that is full of understanding, because it has been through hard places itself; wonderfully patient, because it has a great hope at its heart; utterly pure, because it knows God.

'Judge not, that ye be not judged' (Matt. vii, 1) does not mean (as easy-going good nature might suggest) throwing our critical faculty overboard. (Cf. John vii, 24, 'Judge righteous judgement.') Jesus would have said Amen to the Psalmist's injunction, 'Ye that love the Lord, hate evil' (Ps. xcvii, 10). Leave out the moral stringency of Jesus, and you are not left with the Jesus of the New Testament. In any case, we are to be stern in judging ourselves; as St. Augustine said greatly, 'To my God, a heart of flame; to my fellowmen, a heart of love; to myself, a heart of steel.'

3. Love's Necessity

Wherever Jesus went, He found hearts that were hungry for love. On the jaded face of a Zacchaeus (Luke xix, 5), in the glib talk of a Samaritan woman (John iv, 10 ff), in the weary looks of an inarticulate, shepherdless crowd (Matt. ix, 36), that hunger for love struck at Christ's own heart. Hence He laid it down that, while men did not need many qualifications to be His disciples, no man could be a disciple who was not prepared to love. The heart of the world was crying for love.

According to Jesus, the real foe of God—in Church, in State, in individual—has always been lovelessness. Self is Antichrist. The selfish attitude is one of those respectable sins which (just because they are respectable, as contrasted with certain sins of the flesh) society in Jesus' day and society today have been apt to overlook. Yet to this sin more than to any other, whether of the flesh or the mind, the eyes of Jesus are 'as a flame of fire' (Rev. i, 14). Many things Jesus can forgive: lovelessness He cannot tolerate.

4. *Love's Method*

There is an unkind way of being 'kind', an unloving way of being 'loving'. This was Jesus' charge against the Pharisees. They sounded a trumpet when they did their alms (Matt. vi, 1, 2). Their love was forced. It was professional, official, unnatural. It used words that did not come from the heart. Suffused with a warm glow of conscious virtue, it was none the less counterfeit. It rang false. And the people to whom a love like that was shown could nearly always detect the flaw in it. That was why it hurt them. That was why it was worse than sheer indifference. Real love, said Jesus, makes no parade (Matt. vi, 3, 4; cf. 1 Cor. xiii, 4). It is not a forced nor a patronizing thing, but the natural outflow of a God-filled heart.

Jesus' own attitude is decisive here. His deeds of love were done quietly (Mark viii, 23, 26—note specially 'led him out of the town'; Luke v, 14). His love was never condescending. He loved men, not because it was a duty, but because He could not help it (Mark x, 21). He made Himself their Brother, not because He was in the world to promote brotherhood but because He found them so lovable. Official love is a poor and shabby thing compared with the love of Jesus.

5. *Love's Difficulty*

With Jesus' law of love itself, the disciples most heartily agreed; the trouble began when they tried to apply it in the practical relationships of life. It is there that the trouble always begins. Let us get this clear. We agree with Jesus that love is the greatest thing in the world (Matt. xxii, 40); but if in home or business we are irritable, then our religion is thoroughly unreal. We may assent to every word Jesus says in the Gospels about forgiveness; but if we cannot forget that So-and-so once slighted us, or neglected to consult us sufficiently, or said something hard about us, we are nowhere near Jesus at all. Even in the first disciple band love sometimes broke down. Questions of precedence divided them (Matt. xviii, 1; Mark ix, 34; Luke xxii, 24). Rivalries sprang up (Matt. xx, 21, 24). There was a day when not one of them would stoop to wash the others' feet (John xiii, 4, 5). Feelings of independence and personal rights asserted themselves, and love was ousted.

Jesus' attitude to this matter of independence is perfectly clear. It is the antithesis of the world's attitude. The world says that to declare, when someone has hurt you, that you are going to stand up for your rights and 'get even' is to show your independence. Jesus says it shows a radical lack of independence. It shows you are not independent enough to rise above the hurting thing. You are its slave, not its master. This is the teaching of the Sermon on the Mount (Matt. v, 38-48). It is the teaching of Christ's whole life, 'who when He was reviled, reviled not again' (1 Peter ii, 23; cf. Mark xiv, 65). When love and personal independence appear to collide, it must be a false independence; and there cannot be a moment's doubt as to which of the two things —our apparent independence, or Christ's demand of love— must give way. But that is where the struggle comes in. That is one of the difficulties of love.

Another difficulty, very real to the first disciples and very real today, is this. Can men really live by the law of love, as Jesus pledged His followers to live, in a world where that law is not acknowledged? Can they take that risk?

Clearly if all men everywhere were to agree to accept Christ's command, and were to begin simultaneously putting that command into practice, the practice of it would be easy. But dare Christians begin now, in a world that has no intention of beginning? It would not be nearly so hard for one man here to act lovingly towards another there if he could be quite sure in advance that the other would act in the same way towards him: but for the first to act lovingly towards the second, *and risk the rest*—there's the rub. But certainly it was nothing less than that that Jesus asked. His own love never waited to be sure. It plunged right in. It took the risk. It was while we were still enemies, says St. Paul, that He died for us (Rom. v, 10). It was on the Cross where the world killed Him that He pled for the world's forgiveness (Luke xxiii, 34).

This is a main part of the *adventure* of Christianity. Living by love in a world like this is bound to be a risk. And Jesus never tried to conceal the risk of it (Luke xxi, 12). He made the very risk of it His challenge, especially to youth. Everything that was honourable and gallant in youth, He felt sure, would rise to the challenge. And He was not disappointed. It did rise to it. It is rising to it today. Love's difficulty is love's glory.

6. *Love's Length*

The test of love is the length to which it is prepared to go. Christ's own love went the length of Calvary. And when He bade Peter forgive his brother, not seven times, but seventy times seven (Matt. xviii, 21 f), He meant that true love would acknowledge no limits whatever. Did Christ here ask too much? Did He pitch His demands too high? The criticism has been urged that Jesus' teaching on love is idealistic, impracticable for this rough competitive world, not humanly possible. To that criticism the Gospels return two answers. On the one hand, a Christian exists to attempt the impossible (Matt. xix, 26; Mark ix, 23). On the other hand, the complaint that Jesus expects too much of human nature, and that there are lengths to which it is not 'humanly possible' for love to go, is beside the point. Jesus never said that His religion would be human in that sense. He never suggested that His demands would be humanly possible (Matt. v, 20, 48). He said that the glory of His religion was that there was something in it not human at all, but superhuman, and that it would set men transcending the humanly possible by an inward urge that was divine. 'The truth is', as H. G. Wells has said, 'the Galilean has been too great for our small hearts.'

Hence the law of love is closely linked with the law of cross-bearing (Matt. xvi, 24). Quite frankly Jesus said that any man who accepts the former will sometimes have to face self-crucifixion. And no one has a right to sing, 'Jesus, I my cross have taken,' and yet complain that the law of love and forgiveness unto seventy times seven is asking too much of him. This *is* the cross. Love meant Calvary to Jesus. And 'the disciple is not above his Master' (Matt. x, 24).

7. *Love's Motive*

Jesus never asked His men to do anything for which He did not also supply the power. What He called for, He helped to create. When He laid down the royal law of love, He supplied along with it the necessary dynamic. In the Gospels three master-motives emerge.

Jesus created love *by revealing the essential dignity and lovableness of men*. It is easy to notice a man's shabby coat, his defects in grammar, his peculiar ways: Jesus went deeper, and showed that every soul was a potential son of a King. Of a scorned, renegade tax-gatherer He said, 'He also is a son of Abraham' (Luke xix, 9). A woman whom all good people ostracized He treated with a dignity and courtesy that might have been given to a queen (Luke vii, 37 ff). And when He said, 'Take heed that ye despise not one of these little ones' (Matt. xviii, 10), He was thinking, not only of the children, but of all the weak, defenceless, sensitive things of life. It does most mightily inspire love towards your fellow-men when you can see, as Jesus saw, upon every face that passes you in the street something of the image of God.

Jesus created love *by dying for men*. Every day of His life the disciples saw their Master squandering His strength for the sick and the sinful, and when Calvary came they knew that it was for sheer love of them that He had died. Can you continue to be unloving to any man, even the most unlovable, when you remind yourself, 'It was for that man Jesus died'?

Here lies the real motive for international peace. The man who says he does not believe in peace, who thinks that patriotism means his country before all others, his rights at all costs to be upheld, even though it means trampling some-one else's rights underfoot—that man is not only guilty of foolishness: he is guilty of making the Cross of Christ of none effect. For it was on that Cross that Christ died for love of men. Hence in our generation the work of peace must be something more than the mere hobby of a group of Christians: it is every Christian's plain duty to Christ. And the Cross is the motive and the driving-power.

Jesus created love *by flooding human hearts with His own spirit*. Forgiveness to seventy times seven might be quite out of the question for a man of Peter's temperament to achieve. But what Peter discovered was that it was not out of the question for *Christ in him* to achieve. He began by trying to make himself love his fellow-disciples, and he found that that way was hopeless. But as the days went on, he allowed Christ more and more to flood his heart, and then love to the brethren came of its own accord. As Temple Gairdner of Cairo put it, changing by a single letter the great dictum of St. Paul, 'Not I, but Christ loveth in me.'

This is still today the crux of the matter. 'Other men', said a brilliant German about Goethe, 'I love with my own strength, but he teaches me to love with his strength.' Is there anyone you think you could never love? But Christ could love him. Why should not Christ in you do it? He teaches you to love with His strength. That is the secret.

8. Love's Power

It was Jesus who first proved that love, which in a world given over to force looks the weakest of weapons, is in reality the strongest. Love gains victories which the hard, critical, censorious attitude never gains. The Pharisaic attitude to shamed and broken sinners never had and never has any redeeming power about it. Indeed, it works all the other way, and serves only to bind on the fetters of bitterness and despair more securely than ever. 'God, I thank Thee', said the Pharisee of Jesus' parable, 'that I am not as other men are, extortioners, unjust, adulterers, or even as this publican' (Luke xviii, 11). That is loveless religion, entirely powerless to bring any soul into the Kingdom. But Jesus loved the publican, and by loving him gave him back his manhood and his self-respect, brought the cowed, shamed soul on to his feet again, put the light of hope into his eyes, and saved him. If Peter after his denial had been met with hard censoriousness, in all probability there would never have been a St. Peter in Scripture today. But the love of Jesus, which even after that most terrible failure went on loving him (Mark xvi, 7; John xxi, 15), lifted him right out of the fearful pit of his sin and the miry clay of despair and set his feet on the rock again. And here Jesus was a pattern for all His followers for ever. Love is not only better than criticism: it is also infinitely more effectual. It is redeeming power.

An old fable tells that in all the world there was only one thing that could melt adamant, one liquid potent enough to dissolve the everlasting rock, and that was blood from a human heart. Is there not something more than a fable there? 'If I go through the fire,' says the St. Joan of Shaw's play, 'I shall go through it to their hearts for ever and ever.' So love takes its very defeats and out of them forges the weapon of victory. It is the weakness of God which is stronger than all the force of men (1 Cor. i, 25).

9. Love's Reward

Love, just because it is love, asks no reward. All that it asks is to be allowed to go on loving more and more. The whole idea of taking the Christian way for the sake of reward is alien to Jesus' mind. 'When ye shall have done all those things which are commanded you, say, we are unprofitable servants' (Luke xvii, 10). Yet a reward there is. Certainly lovelessness reaps its recompense. The hard, censorious spirit reacts upon the man who shows it, and he finds himself at last inhabiting a loveless desert of a world. Moreover, the unforgiving spirit, said Jesus, goes unforgiven, because it is ultimately unforgivable. The great parable of the servant whose debt to the king was remitted, but who would not remit a fellow-servant's debt to himself (Matt. xviii, 23-34), ends with the solemn words, 'So likewise shall My heavenly Father do also unto you, if ye from your hearts forgive not every one his brother their trespasses' (Matt. xviii, 35). The loveless spirit is not excluded, it excludes itself, from reconciliation and fellowship with God.

But if lovelessness 'has its reward', there is also a rich reward for love. Jesus' familiar principle, 'Unto every one which hath shall be given' (Luke xix, 26), holds good here; for love is a creative thing, and reproduces itself in others, and returns to the man who lives by it. Even a cup of cold water, if given for the love of Jesus, brings blessing to the man who gave (Matt. x, 42); for every gift to the least of the Lord's brethren is a gift to the Lord Himself (Matt. xxv, 40). Moreover, to exercise forgiving love, said Jesus, is to put yourself in the way of God's forgiveness: it is to live in the only sphere in which the cleansing pardon of heaven can operate (Matt. vi, 12, 14). But the great reward of the loving spirit is none of God's gifts, but God Himself (John xiv, 23). The man who loves is creating the atmosphere in which the Spirit of God can dwell: and the Spirit comes, and tabernacles in that human life, and makes that soul His home. So love is crowned. The Lord is there.

> We are of Thee, the children of Thy love,
> The brothers of Thy well-beloved Son;
> Descend, O Holy Spirit, like a dove,
> Into our hearts, that we may be as one;
> As one with Thee, to whom we ever tend;
> As one with Him, our Brother and our Friend.

15: JESUS AND SOCIAL QUESTIONS

Mon. Mark x, 13-16   The Hallowing of Childhood
Tues. Mark x, 1-9   The Sanctity of Marriage
Wed. Luke xiv, 16-27
                        Family Claims and God's Claims
Thur. Matt. xiv, 14-21   Jesus' Care for the Poor
Fri. Matt. xix, 16-26   The Danger of Riches
Sat. Luke xvi, 19-31   Dives and Lazarus
Sun. Matt. xxii, 15-22   Jesus and Politics

Paraphrase 18: 'Behold the mountain of the Lord'
Hymnary 349: 'Father, who on man dost shower'

1. The Attitude of the Master

We have now to inquire what we can learn from the Gospels about the attitude of Jesus to the social questions of His day and of our own. Two widely divergent views have appeared. On the one hand, it is suggested that Jesus did not concern Himself with social questions at all. On the other hand, He has been hailed as the world's greatest social reformer. It is necessary to examine these positions.

According to the former, Jesus' exclusive preoccupation was the soul. He taught a mystical piety. He was content to leave material conditions just as He found them. He deliberately refused to take cognizance of any aspects of the life of man in the world except the spiritual. He came, not to save the world as it was, but to save men out of the world. He was not concerned with the redress of social wrongs or the reform of social injustice: His thoughts were moving on another plane. This view has led some of Jesus' followers in every age of the Church to make a complete divorce between their religion and their social duties, with the regrettable result that Christianity has sometimes appeared to those outside to be indifferent or even hostile to reform, and has been accused of buttressing old abuses.

It is a totally mistaken view. Even a cursory examination of the Gospels shows how wide of the mark it is. Jesus came preaching a *kingdom*, and the very use of that idea raised profound social issues. He proclaimed a Gospel of brotherhood. He gathered His first followers into a social unit, with a real communal life. The Sermon on the Mount is full of social teaching. His healing miracles, as we have seen (p. 97), sprang from His passionate desire to help men physically as well as spiritually. The hardships of the poor were never a matter of indifference to Jesus (Matt. ix, 36). True, He declared that 'man shall not live by bread alone' (Matt. iv, 4). But neither shall man live without any bread at all, and Jesus always remembered that; and in the heart of the great prayer which He taught His disciples He found a place for it—'Give us this day our daily bread' (Matt. vi, 11). Man's material wants, so far from being matters of no moment, were actually written upon the heart of God: 'Your heavenly Father knoweth that ye have need of all these things' (Matt. vi, 32). Indeed, the whole tendency to distinguish between sacred and secular concerns in life is thoroughly alien to the Gospels. Jesus claimed the whole of life for His province. His religion was to invade every corner of a man's experience, every department of public and private life, every nook and cranny of the world. Everything was to come under the sweep of the one Spirit. No man was to be able to draw a line and say, 'Here Christ's authority stops. Thus far, Jesus, no further. The rest is beyond your sway!' Dual control of that kind, Jesus insisted, would always imply a radical insincerity. For there cannot ultimately be two kinds of truth: there is only one. Either Jesus must be King everywhere, or He has no place at all. The only alternatives are to apply His religion to every single one of life's relationships, or else drop that religion altogether: there is no third option. This is the whole trend of Jesus' teaching in the Gospels. This is the claim of Christianity.

The view which regards social questions as outside Jesus'

scope must accordingly be abandoned. But equally wide of the mark is the opposite view, which hails Jesus as primarily a social reformer. This view holds that the first step towards a redeemed humanity must be a redeemed social order. Improve external conditions, it says, and then the Spirit of God will have a chance. Eliminate poverty and ignorance, and then it will be comparatively easy to eliminate sin. But quite certainly this was not Christ's line of approach. For one thing, Jesus was quite clear that the Kingdom could never be built by human effort: it was to be the act of God. Moreover, Jesus saw, and openly declared, that changed conditions were futile apart from changed hearts (Matt. xv, 19 f). Hence His refusal of the short-cuts suggested by the Tempter in the wilderness (Matt. iv, 1 ff). Men would never be right with one another until they were first right with God. The real trouble of humanity was too deep-seated to be reached by any social remedies or improved conditions; and if Jesus was a great reformer, it was because He was a Saviour first.

Somewhere between the two views we have examined the real truth of the matter lies. Jesus came with a social message for His age and for every age. But the basis of that message was not social, but religious. His influence upon world conditions has been a consequence of His revelation of God. He headed no social revolution, and He legislated for no current social problems: but He brought and imparted a spirit that was bound to set men crusading against social injustice everywhere. It is in this way that Jesus has been the driving power of all noble social service for nineteen centuries. The Spirit of Jesus touched the infamy of the gladiatorial shows, and shrivelled that relic of barbarism out of existence. The Spirit of Jesus touched the institution of slavery, laid the axe to the root of that accursed tree whose branches had been darkening the heavens and robbing millions of God's good sunshine, and down the tree came crashing. The Spirit of Jesus, working through Lord Shaftesbury and others, touched the appalling factory conditions of the nineteenth century, and showed them up, and put something better and more decent in their place. The Spirit of Jesus touched the tragedy of unrelieved distress and pain, and everywhere hospitals and homes of healing sprang into existence; every infirmary in the land today has been built by Jesus Christ. Always it has been through changed men that Jesus has changed the world. Always the highest social impetus has had that religious basis. And the Church is not only truest to its own origins and closest to its own Gospel, it is also strongest as a power for social good, when, while speaking out boldly for social righteousness, it concentrates on its own God-appointed task, *and holds up Christ*.

Keeping this in mind, we shall now look briefly at one or two of the great social relationships on which the life and teaching of Jesus have cast a light.

2. *Family Life*

Jesus Himself belonged to a people among whom the institution of the family was more highly honoured than in any other nation of the world. Various causes had contributed to this high estimate of the family among the Jews. One was the conviction that family life was a divine creation: the prologue of Genesis preserved the story of its origin, and showed that it sprang straight out of the mind of God (Gen. i, 26; ii, 18). Hence it became natural to regard each separate family as a religious organism; and, in a very deep sense, every Jewish father was a priest in his own home (Deut. xvi, 11). Moreover, the Jewish law had played an important part in maintaining the purity of family life. Admittedly the law, in many of its aspects, was a yoke of bondage; but it stands to its credit that it did preserve Judaism from the moral landslide which was happening throughout the rest of the world. Nor must it be forgotten that many a Hebrew mother cherished the secret hope that her son might be the Messiah. This was a favourite interpretation of certain Old Testament prophecies, and it is obvious that such a hope must have helped mightily to keep family life sound and pure.

But Jesus invested family life with an even deeper sanctity. He did this in three ways.

He Himself lived for the greater part of His life in the heart of a family (see p. 27). He had four brothers and at least two sisters (Matt. xiii, 55 ff). For thirty years the glory of God was content to tabernacle in a peasant home. Hence family life has been hallowed for ever.

Further, *Jesus regarded the family as a miniature of the Kingdom of God.* This comes out in His constant use of family relationships to illustrate and drive home some of His profoundest spiritual truths. It was from the life of the family that Jesus drew His supreme conception of the divine nature: God, He said, is a Father. The greatest of all the parables is a story of home-life (Luke xv, 11 ff). Forgiveness as experienced within the intimate relationships of home is a wonderful interpreter of the forgiveness of God. The human family becomes a microcosm of the heavenly Kingdom.

Finally, *Jesus deepened the sanctity of the family by what He did for womanhood and childhood.* Here it is not so much definite teaching of Jesus that we have to go upon, as His whole attitude. By His attitude to the women of the Gospel story, Jesus has emancipated womanhood and crowned it with dignity and honour. Even the lofty Jewish standards were far transcended here. Of marriage, Jesus said, 'What God hath joined together let not man put asunder' (Mark x, 9). Paul was thoroughly true to the spirit of his Master when he declared that in Christ 'there is neither male nor female' (Gal. iii, 28). Childhood, too, came under Jesus' transfiguring touch. There was a day when He 'called a little child unto Him, and set him in the midst' (Matt. xviii, 2); and the child-life has been in the midst ever since. How vast the revolution there has been may be strikingly illustrated from the contents of an old papyrus letter, dating from the beginning of the Christian era, which has come to light during recent excavations. It is a letter written by a husband on foreign service to his wife at home, and its exact date is, significantly, the year 1 B.C. 'Let me tell you that we are still in Alexandria. I beg you to look after the child, and as soon as we get wages I will send you something. If it is a boy, let it alone. If it is a girl, throw it away.' Into a world tolerant of that utter callousness came Jesus, and, taking childhood to His heart, declared that of such was the Kingdom of God (Mark x, 14).

But while Jesus thus deepened immeasurably the sanctity of family life, He was careful to point out that, in certain circumstances, the claims of home must needs be relegated to a secondary place. There came a point in His own life when the home of His youth in Nazareth could keep Him no longer, and the clinging hands had to be gently set aside. Later, when His mother and brethren sought Him out and begged to speak with Him, He could only answer, 'Whosoever shall do the will of My Father, the same is My brother, and sister, and mother' (Matt. xii, 50). Nor did He hesitate to ask a similar renunciation from the men He chose as disciples. On one occasion, describing the disruptive effect His challenge would have on human society, He said, 'I am come to set a man at variance against his father, and the daughter against her mother, and the daughter-in-law against her mother-in-law' (Matt. x, 35). When a potential recruit to His cause made the suggestion, 'Lord, I will follow Thee; but let me first go bid them farewell which are at home at my house,' Jesus, seeing apparently the timid resolution which the entreaties of home would all too easily break, refused the proffered service and turned sadly away (Luke ix, 61). Great as Jesus recognized the claims of home to be, He never hesitated to assert that if ever these claims and the claims of God should be at variance, God's claims must come first. The practical bearings of this demand, in the early days of Christianity, when the new religion was making its way and families were divided over it and persecution was hot, were obvious and far-reaching, as they still are in heathen lands where the Gospel is proclaimed today. But even in our own Christian land and in our own lives, this ruling of Jesus carries weight. When lesser loyalties conflict with larger, He says, a man must see to it that the latter prevail. A Christian must be ready, if God so guide him, to surrender even the call of home for the Kingdom's sake.

3. Wealth and Poverty

The frequency of allusion in the Gospels to money may at first sight seem surprising. Take the parables. Here is one about a wealthy landowner whose profits had grown so embarrassingly large that he found the disposal of them a real problem; the parable relates how he solved that problem to his own satisfaction, and what God thought about his solution (Luke xii, 16 ff). Here is another about a money-lender whose junior assistant, having turned out to be a lazy, good-for-nothing scamp, was about to be dismissed, but managed by altering certain accounts to ingratiate himself with some of his master's influential customers; and the parable ends with the strange saying about 'making friends with the mammon of unrighteousness' (Luke xvi, 1 ff). Here is another about a wealthy Syrian Jew, an honest, decent man in his own way, but far too busy managing his own affairs and entertaining his own friends to have any thoughts for a beggar lying at his back door (Luke xvi, 19 ff). And in all the following parables money finds a place: the Hidden Treasure (Matt. xiii, 44 ff), the Unmerciful Servant (Matt. xviii, 23 ff), the Labourers in the Vineyard (Matt. xx, 1 ff), the Two Debtors (Luke vii, 41 ff), the Good Samaritan (Luke x, 30 ff), the Lost Coin (Luke xv, 8 ff), and the Ten Pounds (Luke xix, 11 ff). Quite apart from the parables, too, money enters largely into the Gospel story, notably in such incidents as the interview with the rich young ruler (Matt. xix, 16 ff), the conversion of Zacchaeus (Luke xix, 1 ff), and the gift which the poor widow made to God (Mark xii, 41 ff).

Now this frequency of allusion might seem surprising until we remember how inextricably the whole question of money gets mixed up with the lives and experience of ordinary men and women in this world, even against their will. It gets mixed up even with fine, spiritual things—like the love of parents for their children, or the compassion of a Good Samaritan for the distress of his neighbour, or the thank-offering a man makes to God. Now Jesus was no fanciful dreamer, dwelling in the clouds: Jesus was a realist, and saw the facts as they were. Here, then, was a whole aspect of life which could not be ignored. Here was a clamant need for all the guidance He could give. Let us see the direction which that guidance took.

It is clear, to begin with, that *Jesus did not say that possessions of any kind were necessarily and instrinsically wrong*. Among His own followers He numbered at least one rich man, Joseph of Arimathaea (Matt. xxvii, 57 ff), and His circle of friends included some who, if not wealthy, were certainly quite well-to-do—such people as Nicodemus (John iii, 1 ff), and the centurion of Capernaum (Luke vii, 2 ff), and the family at Bethany (Luke x, 38 ff), and His nameless host in Jerusalem (Mark xiv, 13 ff), and the women who 'ministered unto Him of their substance' (Luke viii, 3). The moral of the tale of the Rich Man and Lazarus, as Jesus told it, was certainly not that the rich man was sent to torment for being rich, and the poor man rewarded with heaven for being poor: Lazarus was in Abraham's bosom in heaven, and Abraham was one of the richest men who ever lived (Luke xvi, 19 ff). And when Jesus demanded of the rich young ruler that he should sell everything he had and strip himself bare of all possessions, He was not laying down a universal law, but He was striking at the thing which in this particular case happened to be blocking a soul's road to the Kingdom (Matt. xix, 21). Jesus did not say that all possessions were intrinsically evil.

Nor did He teach that poverty is necessarily blessed. Certainly Jesus was poor Himself. He was a homeless wanderer (Luke ix, 58). He had to borrow the coin He used for an illustration (Matt. xxii, 19). When He died, He left no possessions behind Him for men to divide, except the robe which He had worn (Matt. xxvii, 35). They buried Him in another man's tomb (Matt. xxvii, 60). But the poverty of Jesus, like the poverty of His own great follower of a later day, Francis of Assisi, was a noble, liberating thing, full of the beauty of the songs of birds, and the flowers, and the flying clouds, and the open road, and the grace of God. Very different is the poverty of an industrial civilization, with all its attendant miseries of sordidness and squalor. No glorification of this can be found in the Gospels. The Spirit of Jesus is at work in the world to end such misery, and to secure to every man the opportunity of fulness of life. No unbiassed student of the Gospels can fail to see that, while Jesus stood apart from economic disputes, His constant insistence on love and brotherhood implied, in the economic sphere, a demand that the gifts of God which men possessed should be distributed in such a way that all God's children might share the privilege of a life full and free and satisfying. This demand is plainly involved in the very nature of the Gospel. It is an inescapable part of Christ's meaning for the world.

On the positive side, Jesus taught that *possessions must always be regarded as a sacred trust*. Every man is accountable to God for the use which he makes of them (Luke xix, 12 ff). Everything we have received is from God (Matt. v, 45). We are all God's stewards. Nothing is more certain to bring God's judgement and condemnation in the end than a selfish attitude to the good things of this world (Matt. xxv, 41 ff).

Jesus always insisted that *if a man's possessions are beginning to injure his soul, drastic sacrifices are necessary*. Better cut off a right hand than quench the Spirit. Better go into the Kingdom of heaven a pauper, than die a rich man with a pile of gold and a shrivelled, beggared soul. 'What shall it profit a man, if he shall gain the whole world, and lose his own soul?' (Mark ix, 36).

Jesus held that *it was easier for a man to be a Christian, if he did not have many possessions*. Wealth might not be unlawful, but certainly it was dangerous. Riches might be nobly and worthily used, but it took a special measure of God's grace to do it. It is here that the main emphasis of Jesus' teaching about money falls. Again and again it is the peril of the thing that He dwells upon. It is apt to give a man a false sense of security. It indisposes him to the acceptance of a sacrificial life. It tends to tone down his moral standards and blunt the edge of conscience. It may become a man's masterpassion, a thing he bows down to and worships, thus usurping the place of God Himself. There is no mistaking the note of solemn warning in the words, 'It is easier for a camel to go through the eye of a needle, than for a rich man to enter into the kingdom of God' (Matt. xix, 24). Riches, said Jesus, are a terrible temptation: thank God if you do not have to meet it!

Finally, Jesus always reminded men that *the best things in life cannot be bought or sold*. He said that 'a man's life'—the inmost secret of existence, the radiant, throbbing splendour that God intended for all His children—'consisteth not in the abundance of the things which he possesseth' (Luke xii, 15). You cannot buy love, or a quiet conscience, or the laughter of little children, or the care of the heavenly Father. The great things, the things that make life, are not for purchase; they are 'without money and without price', and have nothing to do with wealth at all. But they have everything to do with a man's self-surrender to God and his acceptance of the yoke of Jesus.

4. *The State and Politics*

Here the crucial passage for consideration is the story of the Pharisees' challenge to Jesus on the question of the tribute-money, leading up to the memorable declaration about Caesar's rights and God's (Matt. xxii, 15 ff). Let us examine the incident.

The question put to Jesus was a deliberate trap. 'Then went the Pharisees', says the Evangelist, 'and took counsel how they might entangle Him in His talk.' Their idea was that if only they could drive Jesus into an obvious inconsistency and contradiction, they would greatly discredit His cause. They were not concerned to get at truth: their one aim was to down their opponent. And no doubt the task seemed easy enough. After all, was not Jesus an unlettered peasant? Would it not be a simple matter to lead Him out of His depth? They baited their trap with flattery. 'Master,' they began, 'we know that Thou art true, and teachest the way of God in truth.' They had yet to learn that the keen eyes of Jesus could pierce any mask! They brought out their problem. 'Is it lawful to give tribute unto Caesar, or not?

Ought we to pay the civil tax?' The trap had been cleverly devised. It seemed that, whatever answer Jesus might choose to make, they had Him caught. They saw that if Jesus answered 'Yes', the chances were that loyal Jews, smarting under Roman taxes and reparation burdens, would be finished with Him at once. On the other hand, if He answered 'No', He would be open to a charge of sedition, and Rome would no doubt suppress Him. Moreover, if He kept silent, the people around would naturally construe it to mean that He did not know, and that therefore He was not a real prophet at all. Or if He hesitated, and asked time to consider the matter, telling them to return next day for an answer, that, too, would undermine His influence altogether. The trap had been most subtly prepared. But Jesus broke right through it and discomfited them. 'Show Me the tribute money,' He demanded. And when the coin was presented, 'Whose is this image and superscription?' He asked. 'Caesar's' was the answer. 'Render therefore unto Caesar the things which are Caesar's, and unto God the things that are God's.' Give Caesar what belongs to him: give God what belongs to God.

That great saying has suffered from many strange interpretations. Some have founded on it a theory of the divine right of kings. Others, at the opposite extreme, have argued from it that the State has no rights at all over the truly religious man. Others, missing the whole point, have treated it as an evasion. What is the true interpretation?

One thing is immediately clear. *Jesus was here refusing to give a cheap, one-sided answer in the debate on party politics.* To have been a combatant in that arena would almost certainly have meant giving His message to the world a partisan appearance, thus obscuring the essential revelation He came to bring. Moreover, the political situation of His age, as of every age, was transient and ephemeral, and His purpose was to set it in the light of certain eternally valid laws. In any case, guiding principles, not detailed instructions, were Christ's concern, and His presence amongst men had a loftier aim than the ending of political debate or the finalizing of economic programmes. He came to impart to men a spirit by the power of which they would settle their own debates and work out their own programmes. For the Christian, this of course implies involvement on the political and economic levels.

But while Jesus refused to be drawn into political debate His words, 'Render unto Caesar the things which are Caesar's,' imply that *privilege always carries obligation with it*. If you are indebted to the State, then it is a moral duty to honour that debt, just as you would honour any other. The very fact that these men were using Caesar's money implied that they were availing themselves of the services of Caesar's rule: hence, said Jesus, they were bound to accept their responsibility and pay Caesar what they owed him. Privileges of citizenship have corresponding obligations, and Jesus has no approval for the man who declines his civic duties. In short, the issues at stake, under Jesus' touch, cease to be purely political, and are seen to be moral and religious. Duty, wherever it occurs, is a sacred thing, and must be treated as such. 'Render unto Caesar the things which are Caesar's.'

'*And unto God the things that are God's.*' Were Jesus' thoughts going back to the great Hebrew conception of the creation of man—'made in the image of God'? (Gen. i, 27). Tertullian thought so. Caesar's image was on the coin, God's image was on the soul. And however worn and blurred and defaced the human coin might become out in the world's currency, the image of the God to whom it belonged was still there. Thus through all the tangle and undergrowth of the vexed social and political questions of His day, and of every day, Jesus cuts down to eternal fact. He brings everything back to the question of personal surrender. You belong to God, He says. Your bodies, your souls, your minds, your affections—they are all stamped with the divine image. Honour your debt, then! Give God what is His due.

16: THE GATHERING STORM

Mon.	Mark iii, 22-35	Christ Criticized
Tues.	Luke xi, 37-54	The Pharisaic Spirit
Wed.	Matt. xxi, 33-46	The Rejection of God's Son
Thur.	John vi, 60-71	Waning Popularity
Fri.	Matt. xvi, 21-28	The Shadow of the Cross
Sat.	Matt. xvii, 1-13	The Transfiguration
Sun.	Heb. x, 1-13	
		The Acceptance of the Will of God

Psalm xx, 1-5: 'Jehovah hear thee in the day'
Hymnary 501: 'Take up thy cross'

1. *The Shadow of the Cross*

One of Holman Hunt's most famous paintings, 'The shadow of Death', depicts Jesus in the carpenter's workshop at Nazareth. It is the close of day, and the last rays of the setting sun are streaming in through the open door. The young Carpenter, who has been toiling at the bench, raises Himself for a moment from His cramped, stooping position, and stretches out His arms. Just then the dying sun catches His figure and casts His shadow on the wall behind Him; and its form is the form of a cross. It is the artist's striking way of reminding us that right from the beginning of Jesus' ministry death was in the air. From the very start, the end was certain. That indeed is evident to anyone who reads between the lines of the Gospels. In the hour when Jesus, out in the wilderness of the Temptation, flatly and finally rejected the line of compromise, when He settled it once for all that His attitude to the world-powers and to spiritual wickedness in high places was to be one of uncompromising downright defiance (see p. 43), in that hour the shadow of the Cross fell. Even before then, in the quiet seclusion of the silent years, Jesus may have seen that sinister shadow from afar. For as He studied the Scriptures and came to see Himself mirrored in the figure of the Suffering Servant in Isaiah liii, the thought must have possessed Him that to render a perfect obedience to God, to make a full life-surrender, was certain, in a world which denied God and stoned the prophets, to lead to suffering and ultimately to death. The shadow of the Cross was there from the first.

By the time of the great confession at Caesarea Philippi, it was something more than a shadow. Jesus now began to speak quite explicitly about His coming death. Direct and clear as His words were, however, they failed to stab the disciples fully awake to the truth. The thing, to these men, was incredible! It was all against their preconceived ideas and hopes. It must be some strange parable their Master was telling them—not the literal truth. 'Lord,' exclaimed Peter, 'this shall not be unto Thee'; whereupon Jesus, realizing that even His best friends would fain interfere with His doing of God's will, replied, 'Get thee behind Me, Satan!' (Matt. xvi, 23. See p. 41 above). How difficult it was for Jesus to get them to grasp the dread truth may be seen from the fact that after all this they could still go on babbling about the best places in the kingdom (Matt. xviii, 1; xx, 20 ff), and even more from the fact that when the blow did fall it found them amazed and staggered and utterly despairing (Matt. xxvi, 31, 56). Only Christ saw the Cross steadily, and went unwavering to meet it.

2. *The Opposition of the Pharisees*

We have now to watch the gathering storm, and to probe the motives of the hostility which culminated at Calvary. Let us look first at the Pharisees, for it was from their side that the main attack upon the life and character of Jesus was launched.

History has produced some strange anomalies. Never did it produce a stranger than when it decreed that the men who were, outwardly at least, the most religious people in the land should be the head and front of the opposition that compassed the death of the Son of God. The Pharisees, who were the true successors of reformers under Ezra and Nehemiah, had set themselves the task of keeping religion alive and strong and uncontaminated in dark and difficult days, and right well they had acquitted themselves as defenders of the faith. Righteousness was their keynote, the honour of the one true God their constant theme, and their law (as we saw in our discussion of family life) had kept the moral standard high. Yet to Pharisaism Jesus was anathema. Why?

Three sources of their hatred stand out clearly in the story. The first was that *they believed Jesus to be an impostor.* Hopes of a Messiah ran high among the Pharisees, and when Jesus sprang to sudden popularity they could not ignore Him. Even though He did not openly declare Himself, His movement seemed to be assuming Messianic proportions. But the possibility that the Deliverer of Israel might arise, as Jesus had arisen, from the ranks of the poor, the idea of a Leader who did not share their own background of culture and ecclesiastical tradition, never entered their thoughts. Moreover, the Master's choice of followers immediately condemned the whole movement in Pharisaic eyes. A cause that numbered a Matthew—a renegade hireling of the foreigner—among its chosen adherents was obviously not only open to suspicion: it was not even respectable! People whom any sensible Pharisee would quite definitely have discouraged and held at arm's length were openly welcomed by this indiscriminating Jesus. It almost looked as if He had more interest in the riff-raff of society than in religion's acknowledged leaders! The conclusion was obvious, written as plain as day all over the revival movement the prophet of Galilee had started—the man was an impostor.

Here we see the distinctive Pharisaic sin in action—the sin of scorn. Jesus once told a story which had two characters in it, a Pharisee and a publican. 'God, I thank Thee', said the Pharisee, 'that I am not as other men are' (Luke xviii, 11). That was the Pharisaic spirit exactly. The sin of the Pharisee was the deadly sin of the superior person. And the worst of that superior feeling was that it came out chiefly in spiritual things: his pride was that most devastating and soul-destroying and godless thing—pride of goodness, pride of grace. Blinded by this complacent sin, eaten up by their own self-righteousness, unable to see God when He came to them through ways not of their own narrow conceiving, they pronounced Jesus an impostor, and planned to hurry Him out of the way.

The second element in the conflict between Jesus and the Pharisees was *His attitude to the law and to tradition.* Punctilious observance of all the 613 commandments which made up the Jewish law (and it is significant that of these 613, 365 were negative and 248 positive) was the sum and substance of Pharisaic religion. Orthodoxy declared that these commandments contained the truth, the whole truth, and nothing but the truth. If you had ventured to suggest to a Pharisee that the teachers who had given the law had been dead for years, whereas God was still alive, and that therefore there might conceivably by this time be something to add to it, or if you had hinted to him that a good many of his 613 commandments savoured of an obsolete and pedantic legalism and ought now to be decently buried in order to leave room for new light and truth to come breaking in, he would have held up his hands in horror and called it rank heresy. Jesus took that line, and therefore Jesus was branded a heretic (Mark ii, 18, 24). He came challenging men to rethink God: but that, to the tightly-shut mind of a Pharisee, was preposterous and intolerable. It is a startling thought, but it is written plain across the Gospel story, that a great part of the responsibility for the death of Christ at Calvary must be laid at the door of the sin of the closed mind. 'Surely', said George Meredith, 'an unteachable spirit is one of the most tragic things in life.' It is, indeed. It was an unteachable spirit that erected the Cross.

This aspect of the matter deserves to be emphasized. In every department of life and thought, Jesus is on the side of the open, hospitable mind which welcomes new truth gladly. 'The Lord', said John Robinson, the pastor of the Pilgrim Fathers, 'hath more truth yet to bring forth from His word.' Unfortunately, history abounds in illustrations of Bertrand Russell's saying that 'men fear thought as they fear nothing else on earth'; and nearly every new truth which has won its way in the world has had to begin by fighting for its very life against the determined opposition of those who should have welcomed it. But Jesus stands for absolute honesty of every kind, including intellectual honesty. 'I am the truth,' He said (John xiv, 6). And therefore the obscurantist spirit, the closed mind in every form, is fundamentally irreligious. How ignoble that spirit is stood revealed once for all on the day when it helped to crucify the Lord of glory.

The third charge in the Pharisaic indictment of Jesus concerned His *universalism*. To the average Pharisee, mankind fell into two groups, the one composed of true-born Jews, the other containing all the rest, called indiscriminately and contemptuously 'Gentiles'; and there was an insurmountable barrier between. The very name Pharisee meant 'separated'. Judaism had a monopoly of the true religion. The Jew had vested rights in God. This was the spirit to which Jesus flung down the gauntlet. God, He declared, was everywhere, and for everybody. Despised Samaritans were no whit less God's children than men born and bred in Jerusalem (Luke x, 30 ff; John iv, 4 ff). Of a Roman soldier He said, 'I have not found so great faith, no, not in Israel' (Matt. viii, 10). He drew a picture of a day when all the roads of the world would be filled with marching hosts, men out of every nation under heaven streaming up to the Kingdom of God (Luke xiii, 29). This universalism struck at everything the exclusive Pharisee held sacred and most dear: it was dangerous doctrine, and the Man who proclaimed it must be silenced.

3. *The Opposition of the Sadducees*

Along these different lines the opposition of the Pharisees developed. But they did not stand alone. The Sadducees joined hands with them. Between Pharisee and Sadducee there had often been strain and tension, and sometimes open strife: but common hostility to Jesus bridged the gulf, and made them friends for once. Three things have to be kept in mind in thinking about the Sadducees. They were an aristocratic party, containing members of the old nobility. They were a political party, controlling the nation's interests at home and abroad. They were a priestly party, holding the leading places in the Sanhedrin. The Sadducean spirit was marked by a crass materialism and worldliness. Their outlook on life was utterly secular. Recognizing that their own position depended on maintaining the existing order of things, they adopted towards all new movements, alike in Church and State, an attitude defiantly reactionary. Religion was made subservient to politics. What religion they had was largely of a negative kind, consisting in a denial of certain doctrines which their Pharisaic opponents embraced. They accepted the Jewish law, but denied the accumulated 'tradition' which generations of scribes and Pharisees had added to it. They denied the Messianic hope. They denied the resurrection of the dead and the belief in personal immortality.

It was almost inevitable that the Sadducean spirit and the spirit of Jesus should come sooner or later to open conflict. To this worldly-minded priestly aristocracy, Jesus was definitely a dangerous person: they felt insecure as long as He was at liberty. The danger was not only that His teaching might precipitate a nation-wide movement, which would lead to a clash with Rome, with disastrous consequences to the established political order and to their own comfortable position. There was the further danger which a living religion always occasions to a dead religion. The word of God in Jesus' mouth was like a sword, piercing through shows and shams and unreality. It blazed with honesty. It made insincerity tremble. It was alive, incalculable, life-changing, revolutionary. Hence the Sadducees detested it. They detested even more the Man who proclaimed it. They would have no peace, they told themselves, until the word was silent and the Man was dead.

4. *The Opposition of the Crowd*

Another factor now entered into the situation. There came a

F

point in Jesus' ministry when many of the common people
turned against Him. The enormous popularity of earlier
days began to wane, and the ranks of His admirers and
friends were sadly thinned. How are we to explain this
change in the popular sentiment?

Disappointed hopes partly accounted for it. Seeing Jesus'
mighty works, and listening to His authoritative words,
many of the people had begun to feel that here was the very
Captain they were needing to lead them in their next revolt
and insurrection against the Roman power. And it annoyed
them to see Him apparently squandering His opportunities.
It angered them that He should lose time and be so irritat-
ingly unpractical when He might have been giving reality to
their hopes by smiting a passage for Himself to the throne.
Once, indeed, they came to take Him by force and make Him
a king (John vi, 15). At the very last, the hopes that had been
smothered flared up again in the great Palm Sunday demonstration (Matt. xxi, 8 ff). There can be no doubt that Jesus'
steadfast refusal to fall in with the demand for a national
leader turned a great mass of potential support into open
hostility.

Another factor was *the success of the Pharisees in poisoning the
popular mind*. The Pharisees deliberately set themselves to
sow suspicions of Jesus everywhere. The Galilean ministry
had scarce begun when delegates were sent north from
Jerusalem for this purpose (Mark iii, 22). Wherever in the
story of these Galilean days any traces of opposition appear,
sinister figures can be seen in the background fanning the
sparks into a flame (Mark ii, 6; vii, 1). Now the Pharisees
were the accredited religious leaders of the nation, and their
work of spreading damaging rumours about Jesus naturally
had no small effect upon people who were easily led. It
would have been a simple matter for Jesus, if He had so
chosen, to counter them with their own weapons; but Jesus
would use no weapons but God's, and so the subtle, unholy
influence went on. The poison did its work.

But apart from such causes, many people were alienated
by *the Gospel Jesus preached and the demands He made*. It was no

comfortable Gospel. His demands were imperious. To the
natural man, the Sermon on the Mount, if taken seriously,
was an utterly impracticable programme, and the Master
who proclaimed it an impossible person. A religion which
claimed, as the religion of Jesus did, a full and unconditional
surrender, could never be 'popular' in the accepted sense of
the word. Jesus always told men bluntly that the gate was
strait (Matt. vii, 14). Love to one's enemies, forgiveness unto
seventy times seven—these were the radical, overwhelming
tests He dared to apply (Matt. v, 44; xviii, 22). No half-
measures were to be allowed. 'If thy right hand offend thee,'
He said, 'cut it off' (Matt. v, 30). Discipleship of Jesus, on
these terms, was obviously an affair for heroes. It still is,
and always will be, a heroic thing—a fact which has often
been blurred and forgotten because His own followers have
failed to take Him seriously, and have been content to
acknowledge Him without facing up to His demand for a
full surrender. In Galilean days, the stringency of the Master's demand soon chilled the enthusiasm of many who had
once given Him a rapturous wlecome; and it was of these
that He was thinking when, in one of His greatest parables,
He spoke about the seed in stony places which springs up
quickly and gives real promise, but ere long withers away
(Matt. xiii, 5 f). The very Gospel Jesus preached turned
many from friends to foes. For a world ordered on a selfish
basis will never be able to do anything with God but crucify
Him.

5. *The Hero Christ*

So the shadows deepened and the storm gathered, and Jesus
knew that the hour for which God had appointed Him could
not now be far away. He determined on a bold stroke. He
would meet the opposition at its headquarters. He would
carry the campaign up to the capital. There in the city of
God the final revelation must be given, the decisive blow
struck at the powers of darkness, and the uttermost sacrifice
of redeeming love accepted. 'He steadfastly set His face to
go to Jerusalem' (Luke ix, 51).

From this point on, one steady, dazzling flame can be seen burning through the shadows as they deepened into midnight—the heroism of the soul of Jesus. Listen to His words: 'I have a baptism to be baptized with; and how am I straitened till it be accomplished!' (Luke xii, 50). 'I must walk today, and tomorrow, and the day following: for it cannot be that a prophet perish out of Jerusalem' (Luke xiii, 33). So with high head and steady eyes and firm step He went, with no weapons but His love, no resources but God and His own indomitable soul, to where the entrenched and embattled forces of evil were waiting for Him. No wonder the Evangelist, describing one stage of that last march, has put it like this: 'Jesus went before them: and they were amazed; and as they followed, they were afraid' (Mark x, 32). 'Jesus', says Bengel finely, 'was dwelling in His passion.' If evangelical Christianity, emphasizing (and rightly) the wonderful tenderness of Jesus, has sometimes obscured the blazing heroism of the Master's soul, here on the road sweeping south out of Galilee towards Jerusalem that heroism must be rediscovered and lay its overwhelming spell on heart and conscience again. And especially today, when a world grown impatient of sentimentalisms and in-sincerities is beginning to realize that religion is not a mass of shibboleths but a brave, glad quality of life; when we are learning that the real saints of the Church are not the feeble, ineffective spirits who wail 'Thy will be done' with a sigh of futile resignation, but the men who shout it like a battle-cry—'Thy will be done!'—and go out to take the Kingdom by storm; not those who shun the hard way, but the men who tread it with a song, the young fellow who is living to God in the difficult atmosphere of office or shop or factory or club, the girl to whom the law of Christ matters more than the law of her social set—in such a day as this, it is a Captain, a Commander, who is needed. Here, on the royal road of the Cross, He stands, the Hero-Christ, a Leader for whom men would gladly die. So the strong Son of God went out to His last crusade.

6. *The Transfiguration*

Just before He left Galilee, a strange event happened which strengthened Him mightily for what lay ahead of Him. Six days after the great self-disclosure at Caesarea Philippi, Jesus took Peter, James, and John to Mount Hermon, and was transfigured before them (Matt. xvii, 1 ff; Mark ix, 2 ff; Luke ix, 28 ff). Shrouded in mystery and difficult to interpret as this wonderful incident must always be, it was certainly no dream or fancy, but a real experience—a spiritual experience of the first order for the three disciples, and an experience of supreme spiritual exultation for their Master. The unseen world, which is after all the most real world, came breaking through while Jesus prayed; and as long before at Dothan a prophet's servant had suddenly caught sight of the horses and chariots of God (2 Kings vi, 17), so the disciples became aware that spiritual hosts were hovering round their Master and themselves and crowding in to their defence. Dimly we can understand the reinforcing effect upon the soul of Jesus when the voice from Heaven cried, 'My beloved Son'. It was the seal of God's approval set upon Jesus' choice of the Cross. It was the assurance that God had a mighty stake in what was happening now upon the earth, and that behind the shadow and thundercloud and threatening tragedy stood power and love eternal, pledged to crown the soul of Christ with victory.

In that holy hour, there shone out upon the face of Jesus a light which the disciples had never seen before. Our familiar hymn says:

> Jesus, these eyes have never seen
>   That radiant form of Thine;
> The veil of sense hangs dark between
>   Thy blessèd face and mine.

But here on Hermon it was as though that veil of sense had been drawn aside by the hand of God Himself, and through the human form of Jesus the very Spirit of the Eternal was revealed. 'We beheld His glory.'

Mystic contemplation, depth of spiritual communion,

ecstasy of soul, power flooding in from on high—all that entered into the experience of that wonderful hour which made the face of Jesus shine more brightly than any angel's. But there was another element, too, in the Transfiguration which no careful reader of the Gospels can miss. Here on the Mount Jesus made a new and final consecration of Himself to the will of God His Father. Here He laid His body and soul on the altar of utter sacrifice. Here He surrendered Himself to the last dread demand of His vocation as Redeemer. What had been begun at Nazareth, and sealed at the Jordan, and deepened through all the Galilean days, was here on Hermon made complete, when with a great passion of joy flooding His being He accepted the Cross. 'Lo, I come to do Thy will, O God.'

This does not mean, of course, that Jesus was 'in love with death'. Very different was His spirit from that which speaks in the lines Keats wrote, listening to the nightingale's song:

> Darkling I listen; and, for many a time
> I have been half in love with easeful Death,
> Call'd him soft names in many a mused rhyme,
> To take into the air my quiet breath;
> Now more than ever seems it rich to die.
> To cease upon the midnight with no pain.

There was nothing of that in Jesus. 'In Him was *life*,' says St. John. He was made for life. He loved life passionately. We do not honour Jesus by imagining that He accepted Calvary easily. He hated death. Death was one of the powers He had come to destroy. But to Jesus, God's will was everything. It was God's will that the world should be redeemed; and if the achievement of that redemption lay on the road of the supreme sacrifice, then—welcome Death! That was Jesus' spirit. He loved life dearly, but He loved God's will far more. And mingling with the ecstasy of the Transfiguration was the joy of an absolute self-consecration, a divine joy whose light in that moment flooded His soul and shone out on His face, and brought His amazed disciples down in adoration at His feet.

Hence from the heart of this mysterious crisis in the life of Jesus, a clear challenge reaches us all. The one thing for which we have been created is the doing of the will of God. Obedience to that will may mean sacrifice, and self-negation, and the hard road of the Cross; but there alone can joy be found, and peace, and a life made radiant and shining like the sun. The road of self-consecration is the King's highway: and we are lost if we are not travelling there.

17: THE LAST DAYS

1. The King enters His Capital

After the crisis of the Transfiguration, Jesus moved on towards the south, preaching and teaching as He went. In many villages of Samaria and Judea lying along the route He proclaimed His message of the Kingdom and healed the sick; and it was most probably during this time that the mission of His seventy followers took place (Luke x, 1 ff). But Jerusalem was His final objective. St. Mark's narrative indeed passes straight from the Galilean ministry to the final week in Jerusalem, but considerations of chronology indicate that a whole section of St. Luke's Gospel (from ix, 51 to xviii, 14) belongs to the interval between. According to St. John's account, twice at least before Calvary, Jesus was actually in Jerusalem, at the feast of Tabernacles in October (John vii, 2, 10), and at the feast of Dedication in December (John x, 22). But it was with the coming of the greatest religious event in the Jewish year, the Passover festival in March, when the Holy City was crowded with throngs of pilgrims from every quarter, that Jesus knew that the decisive hour had arrived.

On the Friday evening, six days before the Passover, He

reached Bethany. The following day, the Sabbath, was spent in quiet rest, and next morning He prepared to enter Jerusalem. Great companies of pilgrims were flocking in towards the city; and others, hearing that the Galilean prophet, whose fame was now nation-wide, was approaching, came out to line the roads and watch Him as He passed. All reserve was now over, and when Jesus entered Jerusalem on that Palm Sunday, He entered it as God's Messiah. That was the meaning of the pageantry of that tumultuous hour, and He openly accepted the tribute. Popularity had waxed and waned but now for a brief moment it was reborn. Suddenly the flame that had died to a cold ember blazed up again. Most of the pilgrims who acclaimed Jesus with their Hosannas were no doubt provincials, His own countrymen from Galilee in the north—an entirely different crowd from the city rabble which was to cry 'Crucify Him' before the week was over. It must not be forgotten that even after the tide of popular sentiment had begun to set against Him, and indeed up to the very last, there were thousands of people to whom Jesus remained a Friend and a Hero—people whom He had healed of bodily diseases, families whose tangled home-life He had straightened out, men and women for whom spiritually He had made all things new. They brought their tribute to Him now. Amid the shouts of the welcoming throng, the King rode towards His capital. 'Blessed is He that cometh in the name of the Lord!'

By this act Jesus declared Himself. No longer, as at the beginning of His ministry, did He withdraw from the plaudits of the crowd. No longer, as in Galilean days, did He hold back the secret of His royal dignity from all save the initiated few. Ringing in His mind were the words of one of the great prophets of His people, words which often from His boyhood days He had pondered—'Rejoice greatly, O daughter of Zion; shout, O daughter of Jerusalem; behold, thy King cometh unto thee' (Zech. ix, 9). At last the old seer's dream had come true. Not for ever should the daughter of Zion have to wait for her Lover and her Lord. Not for ever should the throne of David stand vacant. By

His action on that Palm Sunday, Jesus said in a way more plain than words, 'Behold your King!'

The entrance into Jerusalem was an acted parable. It gave the faithful the sign they had been waiting for. It inaugurated the Master's final mission to His people, and was a fitting prelude to the days of intense activity and emotion which were to follow. It focused the whole city's attention on Jesus, so that wherever He went during that closing week crowds followed Him, and His name was on every tongue. And, not least important, it flung down the gauntlet to His enemies. It defied them. Much they could endure, but this procession through the streets was intolerable. This fanatic and usurper must be put down finally. Jesus in that tumultuous hour was issuing a challenge. Every token of royal honour which He accepted that day gave point to the challenge, and every Hosanna of the crowd drove it home. Let the powers of evil do their worst: He knew His power. He was the Lord's Anointed. He was riding to the throne which God had given Him. He was ready for the last campaign.

But even then, lest the excitement of the hour might revive in the breasts of the crowd those material and national ideas of Messiahship and kingship which were so foreign to His mind, Jesus did something to make it clear that His was no earthly monarchy, but an empire of the spirit: He would have no proudly caparisoned war-horse to carry Him, but only an ass's colt. 'Behold, thy King cometh unto thee, meek, and sitting upon an ass, and a colt the foal of an ass' (Matt. xxi, 5). Moreover, something which happened as the procession moved slowly towards the city must have puzzled and startled any who were imagining that in Jesus they had found another Maccabaeus. Where the winding road crept round the shoulder of Olivet, the city suddenly came into view; and Jesus halted (Luke xix, 41 ff). They saw Him sitting silent and absorbed. They saw Him gazing at the city spread out before Him. And then—to their amazement —they saw tears in the eyes that gazed. Jesus wept! They did not know the reason for those tears. They did not understand how His heart was aching for the stubbornness, the blindness, of the city that He loved. They did not realize how He was foreseeing the day, so soon to come, when fire and sword would seal Jerusalem's fate. They only knew that the Leader, whom they had hoped to see asserting Himself with martial vigour and remorseless might, was weeping. And they wondered. And they were disquieted. When the procession was formed again and moved on, the Hosannas were perhaps a little less convinced. Was this, after all, the King they had expected? But Christ's thoughts were not their thoughts; and when the day was over, and excitement still ran high, He slipped away, to the bitter disappointment and chagrin of those who still hankered after a Messiah who would take the throne by force, and returned quietly to Bethany.

2. *The Shadows Deepen*

On the next two days, Monday and Tuesday, Jesus was again in the city. Fearlessly and without any attempt at concealment He showed what He thought of the unholy traffic that was desecrating His Father's house (Matt. xxi, 12 f). Never did the volcanic element in the soul of Christ blaze out more terribly than in the hour when He stood in the Temple courts with the whip of cords raised above His head, and in His eyes a light before which strong men quailed and a whole jostling multitude was cowed to silence and shrank away. To those days belong also the public controversies with His opponents, notably the discussion on the tribute money, which we have examined in some detail already (pp. 141 ff), and the terrific onslaught on Pharisaic casuistry and hypocrisy (Matt. xxiii) which made the breach complete and sealed His doom.

Two days before the Passover, a meeting of the Sanhedrin was hastily convened to discuss ways and means of suppressing Jesus finally. The Sanhedrin was an aristocratic body, seventy-one in number, forming the General Council of the Jewish nation and also the High Court of Justice, and consisting of chief priests and scribes and elders. As its membership included leaders both of the Pharisees and of the Sadducees, friction and strife often marked its deliberations; but in the matter of Jesus a concordat seems to have been reached, and both parties united in demanding His arrest. How to carry out that arrest was the dilemma. The real difficulty was the mercurial temperament of the crowd. No one knew with certainty whether an open, official move on the part of the Sanhedrin might not precipitate a sudden revulsion of popular feeling in favour of Jesus. It was an awkward problem, demanding careful strategy. But an entirely unexpected solution offered itself when one of the Master's own followers craved an audience of the Court. The man was immediately ushered in. Jesus, he said, could be taken secretly, under cover of the dark. He himself knew his Master's movements in advance. He knew His favourite haunts. He would lead them there, and they would have Jesus at their mercy. So the ugly, treacherous scheme was unfolded. Blood money was given, and the pact was sealed (Matt. xxvi, 14 ff).

3. *The Upper Room*

The Wednesday of that week seems to have been spent by Jesus in seclusion, either in Bethany or among the hills. But on the Thursday evening, at the hour of the Paschal feast, Jesus sat down with His disciples in the guest-chamber of one of His nameless friends in Jerusalem. Only a brief hour or two now, and the storm would break in devastating fury; but here in this quiet upper room the very peace of God was reigning. Here the great Christian Sacrament of all the ages was instituted. Here the deathless words about the home of many mansions were spoken, and the promise of the Comforter was given. And here the Master, eating and drinking for the last time before He died with the men whom God had given Him out of the world, the faithful few who through sunshine and cloud had clung to Him and companied with Him down the years and loved Him tonight most passionately, trysted them to meet Him again and to receive from His hands another cup at the banquet of God in heaven.

It is small wonder that this upper room has been a dearer place to Christendom than all the great cathedrals raised by subsequent ages to Jesus' honour. Its story was not finished when the Master rose from the table there and led His friends out to Gethsemane; it was not finished when the candles were extinguished that night and silence reigned again. For when after Calvary the broken-hearted, leaderless disciples sought a hiding-place and refuge from the threatening mob, it was in this same upper room that they found it. This was the place which witnessed their hopeless mourning for the Master they had lost, and this was the place where that mourning was turned to bewildered, incredulous joy when Jesus came back to them through the closed and bolted door, and revealed Himself risen and alive (John xx, 19). Here, too, it is more than likely, they gathered again when He had ascended to His Father, and here the Spirit fell, flooding their souls with the glory of Pentecost, and giving birth to the Christian Church (Acts i, 13; ii, 1). If the tradition is correct which identifies this upper room with the house in Jerusalem to which Peter made his way on his escape from prison (Acts xii, 12), we should be able to conclude that the 'goodman of the house', who figures so mysteriously in the Gospel story (Mark xiv, 14), was none other than the husband of Mary, the mother of John Mark, the earliest Evangelist. We saw in an earlier study (p. 5) that the 'certain young man' who, according to Mark's Gospel, was present in Gethsemane and escaped with difficulty when Jesus was arrested, may have been Mark himself (Mark xiv, 51). We can imagine him helping his father and mother to prepare the upper room for Jesus and His friends, waiting outside the door while the Last Supper was celebrated that night, and then following the little group out to the garden on Olivet to see what was to happen. Be that as it may, this upper room of many memories will always draw and hold the hearts of Christ's people wherever the Gospel is preached; and every time the bread of our Communion is broken and the wine poured out, we feel that we are meeting with Jesus there.

'This do in remembrance of Me,' said Jesus (Luke xxii, 19). It was the Lord's last wish, and Christendom has always held it sacred. In the simple, yet unfathomably profound, action of the Lord's Supper, faith has been nourished down the centuries, and hope kindled, and love sustained. Three kinds of language are at our disposal when we seek to communicate the thoughts of our hearts. There is the language of words; but we all know how soon this breaks down, and how difficult it is to find any words to carry the deepest things. Beyond the language of words, there is the language of art—including music, painting, sculpture—and this, too, religion needs; but here again there is a limit, where the language of art breaks down. Beyond this point, there remains the language of action: and this alone can convey life's final sanctities. So the Church, at Christ's command, takes the bread, and breaks it, and sees Calvary before its eyes; takes the wine, and pours it out, and remembers the blood of the Cross by which the world is saved. We cannot dwell further here on the meaning of the Sacrament which Jesus instituted in the upper room on the night of His betrayal. (*Christian Faith and Practice*, Craig, Milligan and Baillie, pp. 104 ff, should be consulted here.) Suffice it to say that the Church, in celebrating the Lord's Supper, has always found—and rightly—not only a *memorial*, but a *presence*. It is not we who do anything in the Sacrament. It is God who comes to us in Christ, and makes Himself real to our faith, and blesses us with His cleansing fellowship. 'Here, O my Lord, I see Thee face to face.'

4. *Gethsemane*

When midnight came Jesus rose from the table in the upper room, and led His disciples out to Gethsemane (Matt. xxvi, 36 ff). Lying at the foot of the Mount of Olives, it was one of the Master's favourite resorts; this was not the first time they had retired there together for prayer and quiet. But tonight, leaving most of the disciples at the edge of the wood, asking even Peter and James and John to stay a little distance away—for the burden on His soul was now too heavy to be shared even with those who knew Him best, and His spirit craved for solitude and God—He went forward to pray alone in the dark. He fell upon His knees. He fell upon His face. He lay with His face to the ground. And then—the agony which none may ever comprehend began. 'O My Father, if it be possible, let this cup pass from Me!'

We need not think to fathom the soul of Christ while that agony lasted. Only irreverence would probe for explanations here. But of one thing we may be certain: it was not fear of death that made Jesus shrink. Many martyrs have faced the last hour unflinching, with a song upon their lips—and Jesus was braver than them all. It was not death that made Him cry to God: it was sin. It was the shame of all the world, the burden of all the sons of men, which in that dread hour He was taking upon His own sinless heart. It was the sudden sense of sin's sheer horror and loathsomeness and Godforsakenness. It was, as St. Paul with characteristic daring expressed it, One who 'knew no sin' being 'made sin' for men (2 Cor. v, 21). Deeper than this we dare not seek to go. If Christ in His agony left even 'the beloved disciple' behind, it is not for us to intrude. We can only stand afar off, and hear the cry out of the darkness—'O God, let this cup pass!' But then, listening still, we hear another cry breaking the silence, a prayer calm and resolute and full of the peace of a great acceptance—'O My Father, if this cup may not pass away from Me, except I drink it, Thy will be done' (Matt. xxvi, 42). So the faith which never once throughout His life had wavered remained victor even here.

By this time the disciples, weary in body and mind with the strain of these last days, had fallen asleep. Had they been awake and watchful, they might have seen the lights of torches flickering on the edge of the wood. They might have seen dim figures moving among the trees. But there was none keeping guard. In any case, resistance by force was far from Jesus' thoughts; and when Judas and the Temple police and their attendant rabble came, they found but little difficulty in effecting the arrest. The Master was led away, and the disciples, having lost their nerve completely now, 'all forsook Him and fled' (Matt. xxvi, 56).

5. *The Enigma of Judas*

Before passing to the subsequent events of that night of treachery, we must pause here and consider the man who played the traitor. That one who had been in Jesus' company from the first, living daily under the spell and influence of the gracious presence of the Son of God, should have fallen into this appalling infamy at the end, has seemed to some students of Scripture so utterly incomprehensible that they have been driven to the conclusion that this was no ordinary man at all, but Satan incarnate, a monster in human disguise. Such a reading of the enigma, however, is unsatisfactory: it does justice neither to the point of view of the Evangelists nor to the facts of psychology. We must probe deeper.

There had been a day when Judas, like Peter and Andrew and the rest, had left all to follow Christ. That is a fact of cardinal importance. He forsook home and kindred for Jesus' sake. No doubt hopes of an earthly kingdom played a part in that decision; but over and above these was the fact that the man felt the magnetism of Jesus. The appeal of the young Prophet from Galilee moved him as nothing else had ever moved him in his life before; and when the call came, it found him ready.

Even more important is the fact of Jesus' estimate of Judas. The Master's eye, accustomed to read all kinds of men, detected in Judas the makings of a real apostle; here was a man who had it in him to do splendid service for the Kingdom. Sometimes, indeed, it has been suggested that Jesus gave Judas a place near Himself simply because it was necessary for God's predestined plans that there should be a traitor in the disciple band. It cannot be too strongly insisted that any such theory is both absurd and irreligious. It turns predestination into fatalism. It is a slander on Providence and on God's ordering of the world. It degrades the sacred narrative to the level of solemn play-acting. No,

Jesus called Judas to be a disciple for the same reason for which He called the other eleven. He saw in him a man of noble promise and boundless possibilities. No doubt He saw other things as well—moral contradictions jostling one another in the man's secret soul, strange conflicts of light and darkness, courage and cowardice, self-surrender and self-love. But that simply meant that he was a man of human passions; and it was out of such materials that Jesus fashioned His saints. He hoped to do it here. Judas, when he first became a disciple, was a potential man of God.

To begin with, all went well. He was out on the great adventure of his life, and he knew it. But gradually a subtle change came over him. It was as if the spring had gone out of the year. He was less comfortable with his Master now than formerly. The other disciples may never have noticed that anything was happening, but Jesus did. Jesus' secret midnight prayers at this period must have been burdened with Judas's name. The change in the man's attitude seems to have been a direct outcome of Jesus' constant endeavour to spiritualize His followers' earthly and material Messianic hopes and of His failure to take the tide of popularity at the flood. To Judas, such dilatory and unpractical ways were inexplicable and unpardonable: the flood-tide might have led them all on to fortune and spectacular success, but now the chance was lost for ever, deliberately thrown away, and his heart was sore and aggrieved and turning bitter.

This suggests the real motive of his foul deed of treachery. Various motives have been canvassed. *Was it love of money?* That there was a streak of covetousness in his nature is pretty certain, and he seems to have indulged in petty pilfering. One of the Evangelists says bluntly that he was a thief (John xii, 6). But it is hard to believe that money was the master-passion for which he sold his Lord. He could so easily have driven a better bargain with the priests, if that had been his object! The thirty pieces of silver might have been doubled or trebled.

Was jealousy, then, the motive? This, too, may have played a part. The fact that he was the only Judean among the

Twelve, all the rest being Galileans (Iscariot means 'the man from Kerioth', a village of Judea), may have tended to make him solitary and aloof and critical; and we can well believe that, to a man of his ambitious nature, Jesus' choice of Peter, James, and John to form the inner circle of the disciple group (Mark v, 37; ix, 2) must have rankled. But jealousy alone will not explain his crime.

Another theory suggests *fear as the motive*. According to this, Judas saw disaster impending, and realized that when the crash came it would involve not only the Leader of the cause, but all His followers as well: when Jesus went down, He would drag the rest down with Him. The frightened disciple saw that the only way to secure himself and save his own skin, when the worst came to the worst, was to turn king's evidence, in the hope that the authorities, grateful for the help he had given them to lay hands upon their main enemy, would let the informer go free. Certainly we cannot rule this motive out. Yet it does not cover all the facts.

De Quincey made the famous suggestion that Judas played the traitor *in order to force Jesus' hand*. Writhing with impatience as he watched his Master apparently squandering one opportunity after another of asserting Himself and claiming the throne, Judas at last decided that if Jesus would not take action of His own accord, He would have to be compelled to act. But how? Obviously the way to do it would be to get Jesus into a compromising situation. Then He would be forced to bestir Himself and manifest His power. Then the kingdom would come. It is an ingenious theory, and if accepted, it would go far to rehabilitate the worst reputation in history. But it will not hold water. It represents Jesus as an irresolute, procrastinating Hamlet. In place of Judas the traitor, it gives us Judas the misguided saint. Instead of a deep-dyed crime, it speaks of an error of judgement. There is not a scrap of evidence for this in the Gospels. It is quite inconsistent with the words of stern condemnation which Jesus Himself used about His disciple's deed. An error of judgement, the rashness of a too enthusiastic follower, Jesus would certainly have pardoned. But of Judas He could only say—'Woe to that man by whom the Son of man is betrayed! Good were it for that man if he had never been born' (Mark xiv, 21). No, this explanation must be set aside.

We are left with what was almost certainly the real motive —*the man's bitter, revengeful spirit.* Disappointment of his worldly hopes bred spite, and spite deepened into hatred. Judas kept telling himself that he had been deceived, led on by false pretences, that these years of his life had been wasted, and that all Jesus had done for him had been to land him in desperate trouble; well, he would strike back! He would have his revenge. Besides, he had known for long that the steady eyes of Jesus were reading him like a book, discovering all his secret insincerities of thought and character. Jesus, he knew, saw right through him. And that intensified the man's anger and vindictiveness. He began to toy with the thought of treachery. Once that thought had found a lodging in his mind, the rest of the tempter's task was easy. Soon the thought had become a fixed idea, and the deterioration of his soul was startling in its rapidity. Nothing could save him now, not even the sight of Jesus kneeling before him to wash his feet (John xiii, 5), not the final appeal of Jesus at the supper table (John xiii, 26). By that time, he had sold his soul irretrievably. Only the deed itself now remained. But what evil spirit suggested the signal he arranged with his accomplices that night? It was the crowning touch of horror, the last point of infamy beyond which human infamy could not go, when out in the garden Judas betrayed his Master, not with a shout or a blow or a stab, but with a kiss.

18: JESUS ON TRIAL

1. *The Double Trial*

To understand what happened between Gethsemane and
Calvary, we must try to grasp quite clearly the reason why
Jesus was subjected to a double trial. We call it a trial; in
reality it was an inquisition, and the death sentence, when it
was carried out, was nothing more nor less than judicial
murder. Jesus appeared first before the Jewish Sanhedrin:
this was the ecclesiastical trial. Then He was sent to a Roman
tribunal: this was the civil trial. Had the charge on which
Jesus appeared not been a capital one, the Sanhedrin alone
could have decided the matter, without referring it to Pilate
at all. For in Judea, as in all the provinces of her far-flung
empire, Rome gave the conquered people a fair measure of
self-government; and the judicious application of this Home
Rule principle contributed largely to the maintenance of
peace throughout her dominions. But where death sentences
were involved, as in the case of Jesus, Rome reserved the
final right of judgement to herself. Such cases, after going
through the Jewish court, had to come up again for review
before the Roman authorities, who had the power either to
homologate the verdict already pronounced and execute
sentence on the accused, or to overturn the proceedings alto-

gether and set the prisoner free. This explains what happened on the night of Christ's arrest.

2. *Jesus before Annas*

The Temple police who arrested Him in Gethsemane took Him first to Annas (John xviii, 13). Now this part of the proceedings was, strictly speaking, quite informal and arbitrary. Annas held no official position. But he wielded an immense influence and prestige, and in the Sanhedrin no man's opinion carried greater weight. Twenty years before, he had been high priest, a title which he still received by courtesy; and no fewer than five of his sons had succeeded him in this, the highest position in the land. It is probable that it was Annas who had established, for reasons of personal gain, the traffic of the bazaar within the Temple courts which Jesus had so sternly denounced. He was the evil genius behind the plots that had led to Jesus' capture; and though it was after midnight when the prisoner was brought in, the old man was alert and wakeful and determined to push the case forward without delay. After an informal preliminary inquiry, he sent Jesus on to Caiaphas.

3. *Jesus before Caiaphas*

Caiaphas, Annas' son-in-law, was high priest and head of the Sanhedrin. This was the man who was the accredited guardian of the nation's soul. He had been set apart to be the supreme interpreter and representative of the Most High. To him was committed the glorious privilege of entering once every year into the Holy of Holies. Yet this was the man who condemned the Son of God. History provides no more startling illustration of the truth that the best religious opportunities in the world and the most promising environment will not guarantee a man's salvation or of themselves ennoble his soul. 'Then I saw', says John Bunyan, closing his book, 'that there was a way to hell, even from the gates of heaven.'

News of the arrest of Jesus had by this time been carried round, and had brought many members of the Sanhedrin to the high priest's house. According to its constitution, the Sanhedrin could not legally be convened before the hour of sunrise; but Caiaphas and the rest were impatient of delay, and decided to proceed with the examination of the Prisoner at once. All that would then remain for the formal meeting after sunrise would be the ratification of any decisions arrived at meanwhile at the informal sitting, and valuable time would thus be saved (Matt. xxvi, 57; xxvii, 1). Caiaphas began by putting questions to Jesus about His disciples and His doctrine (John xviii, 19). No doubt he hoped to draw from Jesus some statement of His teaching which could be twisted round to mean that He had anti-Roman sympathies: this could then be used decisively against Him when the trial before the Roman governor began. But this first line of attack failed. 'You know My teaching,' said Jesus in effect. 'I have never made any secret of My beliefs: they are public property. Why ask Me now?' And Caiaphas was discomfited (John xviii, 20). Equally unsuccessful was his second attempt. He brought in witnesses against the prisoner, in the hope that they would produce evidence on which without more ado sentence of condemnation could be passed. But the witnesses failed to agree, and in any case their evidence was of the flimsiest. Again the President of the Sanhedrin had to own himself baulked (Mark xiv, 56, 59). Growing anxious and uneasy at the course which the investigation was taking and at the complete failure of the court to substantiate any charge against the accused, Caiaphas suddenly decided to bring his last and most dangerous weapon into action. Point-blank he demanded of Jesus whether He claimed to be Messiah. Now or never, he felt, Jesus would incriminate Himself! And when Jesus quietly replied, 'I am,' adding significantly that a day was coming when the Son of man would be seen sitting on the right hand of power, the high priest, overjoyed and triumphant that his enemy had given Himself away at last and played into His accusers' hands, cried out that it was blasphemy and that no further witnesses were needed, for the prisoner stood condemned out of His own mouth (Mark xiv, 63 f).

With this the court unanimously concurred, and the death penalty was decreed.

To all intents and purposes the Jewish trial was now over. Formal ratification of the verdict when the Sanhedrin met officially after sunrise would be a matter of only a few minutes. Meanwhile the condemned man could be handed over to the tender mercies of His gaolers and of the mob. Even members of the court took part in the unholy display of cruelty that followed (Mark xiv, 65). It was while this infamy was being perpetrated that there occurred an incident which all four Evangelists record, and which the conscience of the Christian Church has never been able to forget—Simon Peter's denial. Impetuous and devoted to the last, Peter had found his way into the high priest's courtyard. But he had not been there long when he began to rue it. He had an uneasy feeling that he was being watched. There were eyes following him. The place seemed full of eyes. And when the challenge came, sudden and swift and inescapable, he lost his nerve, and clamoured with an oath that Christ had never meant anything to him at all. Just then the guards marched their prisoner past, and Jesus heard. 'The Lord turned, and looked upon Peter. And Peter remembered' (Luke xxii, 61). Sorrow and heartbreak and pain unutterable were in that look, and the shamed disciple stumbled out into the night, weeping bitterly. The story of it stands here for all generations of Christians to read and ponder; for human hearts are the same today as they were then, and all disloyalties to the Master just as dark as Peter's tragic failure, and forgiving love as amazing as when Jesus met His friend again beyond Calvary and bade him feed His lambs.

4. *Illegality of the Trial*

We have now to turn from the ecclesiastical to the civil trial of Jesus. But let us first summarize the points at which the proceedings thus far had offended against the elementary rules of law and justice. In what respects was the Sanhedrin's judgement illegal?

(1) It was illegal in that the court which was to decide Jesus' case was also an accomplice in His betrayal. Members of the Sanhedrin were inextricably implicated in the secret plots that had culminated in Judas's deed of treachery. Yet these same men were now to act as jury. This vitiated the proceedings from the outset.

(2) The trial did not begin, as Jewish law demanded, with a statement of a definite charge against the accused. Indeed, the real difficulty of Caiaphas and his friends, as we have seen, was to find any charge at all on which they could commit Jesus to Pilate. When the witnesses disagreed, and no charge was forthcoming, it was the court's duty to abandon the case. But this was not done; the proceedings were allowed to drag on. This, too, was illegal.

(3) Moreover, the judge trying the case was also leader for the prosecution. Caiaphas combined in himself both these roles. He took his place as president of the court that night, absolutely determined in advance to secure a conviction. Had he not already declared, in one of the most cynical, cold-blooded epithets history has preserved for us, that it was 'expedient that one man should die for the people' (John xi, 50)? When the hearing of witnesses turned out to be a fiasco, the judge himself began putting leading questions to the prisoner. He knew that by doing so he was going dead against the law, but he would rather have broken the law a hundred times over than let Jesus slip through his fingers now.

(4) Further, there were no witnesses for the defence. None were summoned. None had a chance to appear. It was Jesus against the world. No voice was to be tolerated except the voices of the prosecutors.

(5) But the crowning illegality of the trial was the haste with which it was completed. In the dead of night the case was hurried through. The holding of a brief, formal meeting at sunrise to ratify the night's work and to give a faint show of legality to what had been done did not alter the fact that the Sanhedrin's midnight investigation was a flagrant breach

of its own laws. But that was not the worst. There was a law that, in capital charges, sentence of death could be pronounced only on the day after the trial: twenty-four hours had to elapse. There was a further law that such cases were not to be heard at all on the day immediately preceding a Sabbath or one of the great festivals. Both these laws were broken. In desperate anxiety to get Jesus out of the way before there should be any chance of a popular rising in His favour, His accusers flung principle to the winds and tore justice to shreds.

5. *Jesus before Pilate*

When Caiaphas and his satellites had done their work, Jesus was marched off to the Roman governor for the second stage of His trial. Pontius Pilate had now been procurator for six years, and had found the post by no means a sinecure. The Crown Colony of Judea was one of the most difficult and turbulent corners of the Emperor Tiberius's vast dominions. But Pilate's unnecessarily harsh and relentless ways of dealing with the administrative problems that were continually confronting him had made him anything but popular with the people he had to govern. He despised the Jews, and failed altogether to appreciate the religious traditions of their race. They had not forgotten the day when, in open defiance of Jewish sentiment and in flagrant breach of the conciliatory policy which Rome officially sanctioned, Pilate had caused images of Caesar as god to be carried through the streets of the Holy City. Nor had they forgotten certain other occasions when he had read the Riot Act and sent his soldiers in amongst the crowds, and caused bloodshed and massacre (Luke xiii, 1). Neither the Sanhedrin nor the mass of common people had much love for Pilate; but the spur of necessity works wonders, and it was now the main hope of Caiaphas and the rest to make a good impression on their governor and win him to their side, and so secure the death of Jesus.

Pilate began, as was perfectly right, by demanding a definite statement of the charge (John xviii, 29). But this was

extremely awkward. For when the Sanhedrin had convicted
Jesus, it had used, as we have seen, the accusation of blasphemy—a purely religious matter, which was unlikely to
carry much weight with an irreligious Roman or to be
deemed worthy of the death penalty. So the Jews replied
evasively. 'If He were not a malefactor, we would not have
delivered Him up unto thee' (John xviii, 30). Naturally this
did not satisfy Pilate, and he pressed for further information.
Whereupon Jesus' accusers, adding yet another illegality to
all that had gone before, quietly dropped the original charge
of blasphemy and substituted another in its place, one of a
kind of which Pilate would be bound to take cognizance—a
charge of treason (Luke xxiii, 2). They declared, first, that
Jesus was perverting the nation (this was a slander); second,
that He forbade paying tribute to Caesar (this was a deliberate untruth—see Matt. xxii, 21); and third, that He claimed
to be a King (this was true, though not in the sense which
they implied). Having heard this triple charge, Pilate decided
to examine Jesus in private.

No scene in history has impressed itself more vividly
upon the imagination of the world. Reading between the
lines of the narrative, we begin to see that all through that
momentous hour when the judge was deliberating what to
do with this strange prisoner whom fate had thrown in his
way the prisoner was wrestling for the soul of His judge.
Pilate was not a lost man yet, and Jesus would fain have
saved him from himself. Moreover, the governor was quick-
witted enough to see that this was no ordinary wrongdoer
with whom he had to deal; and he could not but be amazed
at the composure and steadiness and dignity and kingliness
of the man in front of him, for whose blood the mob outside
was clamouring. He ended the interview, and went forth to
declare his verdict—'Not guilty!'

But this inflamed the passions of the crowd; and now for
the first time fear and uncertainty began to mark Pilate's
demeanour. He saw trouble ahead, and became anxious to be
rid of this difficult case altogether. In his efforts to evade
responsibility, he had recourse to three expedients. The first

was to send Jesus to Herod (Luke xxiii, 7). After all, he
argued, Jesus was a Galilean, and therefore subject to Herod's
jurisdiction: why should not Herod (who by a great stroke
of fortune was in Jerusalem at the time) accept the responsibility and see the trial through to an end? It was a clever
move; but unfortunately for Pilate it did not work out as he
had hoped. Back to his palace came the escort with their
prisoner a short time later, bearing a message to the effect
that Herod thanked the Roman governor for his courtesy
but would not dream of robbing him of his privilege, and
begged him to finish the case himself. The second expedient
Pilate tried was a dastardly one. He proposed that, as he
could find no fault in Jesus, he would scourge Him and
release Him (Luke xxiii, 16). This sorry compromise was,
of course, totally unjustifiable and illogical. It was the poor,
fear-driven soul's attempt to do his duty by Jesus and to
please the crowd at the same time. But it did neither; and it
is no wonder that the angry priests would not accept that
verdict at any price. The cries of 'Crucify, crucify!' grew
from a murmur to a tumultuous shout. Baulked in these two
attempts, Pilate now tried one last device. He set Jesus over
against Barabbas, and gave the crowd their choice, hoping
against hope that they would prefer that, of the two, Jesus
should live (John xviii, 39). But this also failed, for there
was a loud, acclaiming cry for Barabbas. Pilate was now at
his wits' end, when suddenly a voice called out of the crowd,
'If thou let this man go, thou art not Caesar's friend' (John
xix, 12). And that settled it. For Pilate knew all too well what
that threat meant. The last thing in the world that he wanted
was that a complaint against himself should be sent back to
his imperial master in Rome. Impeachment would mean ruin,
for there were things in his past life which could not bear
examination. Anything rather than that! It was his career
against Jesus. Well, Jesus would have to go. Gladly as he
would have set the man in front of him free, his own interests,
his own bad past, blocked the way, and made the sacrifice of
innocence essential. He yielded to the clamouring crowd,
and sent Jesus to His doom.

6. Jesus as Judge

So the trial, which was no trial, ended. One extraordinary
feature of the whole story let us notice in closing. Everyone
who studies the narratives has the strange feeling that the
tables are being turned before his very eyes, and that what
he is seeing is not Jesus on trial before Caiaphas or Pilate or
Herod: what he is seeing is Caiaphas, Pilate, Herod on trial
before Jesus. And when all is over, and the prisoner has
been marched away to Golgotha, it is not He who has been
judged by them: it is they who have been judged by Him.
Face to face each of them—Caiaphas, Pilate, Herod—stood
with the Son of man for a brief hour, and His searchlight
played upon their souls, revealing their inmost nature, and
showing them up for all the world and for all time to see.
On that dark, crowded night, the real Judge was Christ.
And where Caiaphas, Pilate, and Herod stood that night,
every soul at some stage of its life-journey must stand—face
to face with Jesus, in the place of decision: and each soul's
verdict on the Lord of all good life is, in a deep and solemn
sense, Christ's verdict on itself.

19: CALVARY

Mon.	Matt. xxvii, 27-36	Via Dolorosa
Tues.	John xix, 19-22	The Title on the Cross
Wed.	Luke xxiii, 39-43	The Penitent Thief
Thur.	Matt. xxvii, 39-50	The Last Temptation
Fri.	Luke xxiii, 46-50	Crucified, Dead, and Buried
Sat.	Col. ii, 10-15	The Cross as the Defeat of Sin
Sun.	Rom. v, 1-11	
		The Cross as the Revelation of Love

Psalm xxiii: 'The Lord's my shepherd, I'll not want'
Hymnary 106: 'When I survey the wondrous cross'

1. *The Holy of Holies*

When Moses in the desert drew near to the burning bush, he heard a voice bidding him put off his shoes from his feet, for he was standing on holy ground. Our thoughts are to turn today to Calvary, the holiest spot in all the earth, which none dare approach save in the deepest reverence. In this the Gospel writers themselves are our best example. Feeling that here they were handling a theme too high and deep for human words, the Evangelists have given us a narrative marked by a noble reticence and a perfect restraint. Unutterably poignant and terribly moving their story is, but there is no narrowing of feeling, no working up of emotion: that dignified, reverent reserve characterizes it all. So far from diminishing the narrative's power, this quietness and simplicity intensify its effect immeasurably. To take but one example, where in the literature of the world will you find a sentence burdened with a deeper pathos than this—'Now there stood by the cross of Jesus His mother' (John xix, 25)? How restrained and artless that is, for the Evangelist makes no effort to elaborate it; and yet, in the picture it conjures

up, how overwhelmingly moving! With perfect reverence
the Gospels lead us into the holy of holies of our Lord's
last hours; and in the writers' simple, unadorned words all
Christendom has found 'thoughts that do often lie too deep
for tears'.

2. A Willing Sacrifice

Jesus, as we have seen in our last two studies, was put to
death by a coalition of definite historic forces. Church and
State and people all combined to destroy Him. Pharisaic
blindness and intolerance, priestly exclusiveness and self-
seeking as exemplified in Caiaphas, imperial policy and
power as embodied in Pilate, popular disappointment and
resentment and revenge as seen in the Jerusalem mob—these
were the things which put Jesus on the cross. But it would
be a profound mistake to suppose that these historic forces
were the final, determining factor. Jesus was not driven to
death: He went in the freedom of His own unconquered
soul. It was no helpless victim of cruel circumstances who
died on Calvary; for in that sacrifice, as the New Testament
from first to last insists, Jesus Himself was Priest, and
willingly laid down His soul upon the altar. 'The Son of
man came', He said, 'to give His life' (Mark x, 45). And
again: 'No man taketh it from Me, but I lay it down of
Myself' (John x, 18). An element of necessity there undoubtedly was in the death of Jesus: 'The Son of man', He
said, '*must* suffer, and be slain' (Luke ix, 22). But it was the
necessity, not of violence and constraint, but of His own
consuming love for men. For from the beginning Jesus had
undertaken His work of world-redemption with His eyes
open, knowing full well the price, and willingly accepting it.
Hence His amazing calmness and self-possession as the end
drew near. Never was fancy further from the fact than when
His judges imagined themselves masters of the situation at
last and controllers of His destiny. Jesus, who from the
Galilean days had mastered life and circumstance and every
new emergency, was supremely master in that hour when
He went, not beaten by human malice or dragged helplessly

at the chariot-wheels of fate, but voluntarily and victoriously to the glory of His finished work. This was 'the weakness of God', which 'is stronger than men' (I Cor. i, 25).

3. *The Offence of the Cross*

Here it may be well to remind ourselves of what death by crucifixion meant in the thoughts of the ancient world. With the passing of the years, Christendom has cast a halo of beauty round the cross. We build our churches in the shape of a cross. We emblazon the cross on the flags of the nations. Beneath the cross we bury our dear dead. We take a Red Cross, and with it symbolise the ministry of healing. Our poets and hymn-writers sing to us of 'the wondrous cross', 'the blessed cross'. But all this ought not to hide from us the fact that originally the cross was a thing unspeakably shameful and degrading. 'Cursed is everyone that hangeth on a tree', said Paul, quoting Deuteronomy (Gal. iii, 13; Deut. xxi, 23). That was how Jewish feeling expressed it; and Roman sentiment was the same. 'This cruellest, most hideous of punishments', said Cicero, using words in which you can almost hear the shudder—'crudelissimum taeterrimumque supplicium'. 'Never may it', he said elsewhere, 'come near the bodies of Roman citizens, never near their thoughts or eyes or ears!' Devised in the first instance in semi-barbaric Oriental lands, death by crucifixion was reserved by the Romans for slaves and for criminals of the most abandoned kind. It was a fate of utter ignominy. It was the hangman's rope of the ancient world. Small wonder that when the first Apostles began their world-mission, they found one prejudice everywhere confronting them, among Jews and Gentiles alike—'the offence, the stumbling-block, of the cross' (Gal. v, 11; I Cor. i, 23). That the Messiah should die was hard enough to credit; but that He should die *such* a death was utterly beyond belief. Yet so it was. Everything which Christ ever touched—the cross included —He adorned and transfigured and haloed with splendour and beauty; but let us never forget out of what appalling depths He has set the cross on high.

4. The Cross-Bearer

It was the custom of those days, as a refinement of cruelty and a last master-stroke of vindictive insult, to compel a condemned man to carry his own cross to the place of execution. But when the procession to Calvary had been formed and began to move off down the crowd-lined streets, it soon became apparent to the Roman centurion in charge and to his escort of soldiers that Jesus would not be able to bear His heavy burden all the way. Exhausted by the frightful scourging to which He had already been subjected (for the iron-tipped thongs of the Roman *flagellum* had done their cruel work all too well), the prisoner sank at last to the ground, and the procession was halted. Now no Roman would ever have thought of asking another Roman to shoulder a cross, so great were the pollution and the shame of the thing; and therefore the centurion, passing over all his own men, fixed on a stranger standing by and conscripted him for the unwelcome task (Mark xv, 21). A soul's great hour sometimes leaps upon it, and destiny stands waiting all unexpected at the corner of some common road: so it was with Simon of Cyrene, when he turned aside with idle curiosity to watch a passing crowd, and before he knew what was happening was carrying the cross of the Son of God. No doubt his first feeling was one of anger and resentment that he had been requisitioned for a duty involving such a stigma. But when, long afterwards, he looked back upon that hour, it was to thank God for the crowning honour of his life. 'The father of Alexander and Rufus', Mark calls him, obviously referring to two prominent figures of the subsequent apostolic Church (cf. Rom. xvi, 13); and we cannot escape the conclusion that it was the memory of this hour on the Calvary road when he took the Master's cross that changed Simon's life, and brought him, and his household with him, to the Christian faith. It is not surprising that the figure of this Cyrenian, appearing so abruptly on history's greatest page and then vanishing again, has fascinated the imagination of Christendom, for among all the services rendered by men and women to Christ in the

days of His flesh, this man's service stands alone. Some, like
Martha, could spread for Him a table. Others, like the goodman of the house, could give Him sanctuary when foes were
near. Others, like the woman who was a sinner, could break
their treasures at His feet. But only Simon carried His
cross.

5. *The Title on the Cross*

When the destination was reached, the soldiers began their
work. They laid the cross down upon the ground. They
stretched their Prisoner out upon it, nailing His hands and
His feet. Then they lifted it up, and dropped it into the
socket in the earth. And then, says Matthew, with one of
those vivid touches which say so little but suggest so much,
'sitting down, they watched Him there' (Matt. xxvii, 36).
They watched Him. They were face to face with the event
which was to change the world. They were gazing, had
they but known it, on God's great heart made bare. They
were confronting the very scene to which innumerable souls
now owe their ransom. They were in the immediate presence
of the final revelation. And they saw—nothing. Gambling
and playing with their dice they whiled the slow hours away.
For always there is a moral and spiritual qualification for
recognizing God.

All the four Evangelists record that over Jesus' head, as
He hung dying, there was an inscription. It was a common
custom, whenever a criminal was executed, publicly to
placard the nature of his crime: a brief description of the
charge on which the man had been condemned was nailed
to the gallows itself, in order that passers-by, looking up
and seeing him there, might know what had brought him
to that end. Jesus had been condemned because His claims
to kingly rights were treasonable and constituted a public
danger; and therefore, as the charge and accusation above
His head, it stood written, 'Jesus of Nazareth the King of
the Jews' (John xix, 19). It was Pilate who chose the wording
of it, and we would fain know what exactly was in his mind.
Was the title just a cheap sneer at the carpenter's apprentice

G

whose hallucinations had been His ruin, a last fling at the
misguided soul who had thought to rival Caesar? Or was
it not so much a jest at Jesus' expense as a jest at the expense
of the Jews, whom Pilate despised and loved to humiliate—
as much as to say, 'This is your king, all the king that poor
slaves like you deserve'? That may have been his meaning;
for we are told that when the Jewish priests read the inscription, the veiled insult of it so incensed them that they
went at once to Pilate and petitioned for its removal. But
Pilate only laughed to see them squirming beneath his sar-
casm, and retorted, 'What I have written I have written'
(John xix, 22). And yet, is it not possible that Pilate's meaning went deeper? May it not have been that something of
Jesus' strength and dignity and innate godlike majesty had
laid its spell upon Pilate; that some hint of Jesus' essential
royalty, some inkling of the truth of His incredible claim,
had dawned upon the procurator's soul; and that it was in
obedience to that deep instinct, which he would not have
dared to confess even to himself, that he wrote the words,
'This is Jesus the King'? Be that as it may, we cannot miss
the significance of the fact that the inscription was written
in three languages, Greek and Latin and Hebrew. No doubt
that was done in order to make sure that everyone in the
crowd might read it: but Christ's Church has always seen in
it—and rightly—a symbol of the universal Lordship of her
Master. For these were the three great world languages, each
of them the servant of one dominant idea. Greek was the
language of culture and knowledge: in that realm, said the
inscription, Jesus was King! Latin was the language of law
and government: Jesus was King there! Hebrew was the
language of revealed religion: Jesus was King there! Hence
even as He hung dying it was true that 'on His head were
many crowns' (Rev. xix, 12).

6. *Himself He would not Save*

The Tempter who had assailed Jesus in the desert and
throughout His life was now to launch his last attack. Members of the Sanhedrin, not content with having secured

Christ's condemnation, had come out to Calvary to gloat over His sufferings, and now they began jeering: 'If Thou be the Son of God, come down from the cross' (Matt. xxvii, 40). That was not only a taunt: it was a temptation. It was a double temptation. It was a temptation to leave the last dregs of the bitter cup of suffering untasted, to escape before the uttermost farthing of the price of sin was paid. But it was more. It was a temptation to do something dazzling and dramatic at this eleventh hour to compel men to believe. 'Let Him come down from the cross, *and we will believe,*' cried the crowd. That was the real sting of it for Jesus, for the creating of belief was the aim and object of His life. But now in dying He flung that last temptation from Him, and refused the startling miracle: away back in the desert He had settled it once for all that not by such spectacular ways would His Kingdom come (see p. 41 above). And when in bitter mockery they cried, 'He saved others, Himself He cannot save' (Matt. xxvii, 42), they were saying something deeper and truer than they knew. It was a fact, it was indeed the central fact of the Gospel, that in His passion to save the world by giving the final revelation of love, Jesus would not and could not save Himself. Not by the Roman nails through His hands, but by the perfect love in His own heart, He was bound to the Cross, bound fast to it until the work was done; and His refusal to save Himself has become the saving of the world.

7. *The Dying Thief*

Jesus did not die alone. It may have been a desire on His enemies' part to carry their jests and insults still further which prompted them to hang a thief on either side of Him, but though they did not understand it there was a singular appropriateness in the act. All His life long Jesus had been the friend of sinners, and in His death He was not divided from them. God Himself, when He had first called His Son to be the Saviour of the world, had indissolubly linked together the love of Jesus and the shame of perishing souls: and what God hath joined together, let not man put asunder.

So to right and left of Jesus' cross on Calvary the crosses of the two malefactors stood (Luke xxiii, 33). Who were they—these two nameless souls who have thus been thrust into the gaze of the centuries? Desperadoes perhaps like those who (as Jesus' own story of the Good Samaritan reminds us) infested the Jerusalem to Jericho road. It is more than likely that they were associates of Barabbas the insurrectionist; for the revolutionary movement which he headed, though in its beginnings directed with nationalist fervour against the Roman domination, had degenerated into mere brigandage and crime and murder. Crucified alongside Jesus, both the dying thieves began reviling Him. But something about the Man on the centre cross brought one of them to silence. This Man who had endured and was enduring the frightful agony without a cry, whose bearing even under the shadow of death had something in it strangely royal, who had been praying for the men who drove the nails in, 'Father, forgive them, for they know not what they do'—who could He be? Again and again the thief turned his head to gaze upon that serene and loving face. Who *must* He be? Suddenly out of the depths faith rose and stormed the heights. 'Lord, remember me when Thou comest into Thy kingdom!' (Luke xxiii, 42). It is an amazing tribute to the sheer kingliness of Christ that at the very last, when everything to outward appearance was lost, and pomp and circumstance were nowhere, one man, gazing at Him as death came hurrying on, felt instinctively that He was marching to a throne. 'Verily,' said Jesus, in reply, 'today shalt thou be with Me in Paradise,' thereby setting the final seal to the truth which He had given His life to declare—that in a single moment, from the dust-heaps and cinder-heaps of life, any ruined hopeless soul, bound in affliction and iron, may pass straight to the perfect release of forgiveness and wear the white robes of a saint.

8. *The Swelling of Jordan*

There was one moment during these last hours of agony when even the soul of Jesus trembled, for the Father seemed to have hidden His face. We can never hope fully to comprehend what Jesus' thoughts and feelings were when the cry rang out, 'My God, My God, why hast Thou forsaken Me?' (Matt. xxvii, 46; cf. Ps. xxii, 1). We may say that that dark, mysterious moment was the culmination of His life-long self-identification with men in all the most desolating experiences of their souls: but it was more. We may say that here the unspeakable shame and sickening horror of all the sins of all the sons of men came down overwhelmingly on His own sinless heart: but even that does not fathom the deeps of His bitter cry. We can only stand afar off and bow our heads, and leave Christ to traverse that darkness alone. One thing is gloriously certain, that when He reached that breaking-point of faith His faith refused to break; for when the cry stabbed the silence, it was 'My God, My God' still.

Beyond that cry there came another, like a victor's shout this time—'It is finished!' (John xix, 30). That, indeed, was no more than what everyone else on Calvary was saying then—but with what a difference! It was finished for the soldiers, and they could go back to their barracks now. It was finished for His mother and Mary Magdalene and the poor remnant who had loved Him to the end, and they could go wearily back to a world that would never be the same. It was finished for the jesting priests and the rabble mob, and they could congratulate themselves that their vengeance was complete. But when the man on the centre cross suddenly raised His resolute eyes to the sky, and cried with His dying breath, 'It is finished!' the whole kingdom of darkness must have trembled to its foundations. For it was not only the long strain of life, with its turbulent close, that was finished now for Jesus, nor was this a mere sigh of relief. The work was finished, Satan's empire was finished, the redeeming of the earth was finished; and this was a triumphant assertion of achievement, this was a conquering shout. With that glad cry the soul of Jesus burst home into His Father's presence. He had glorified God on the earth; He had finished the work which God had given Him to do.

9. *What the Cross Means for the World*

Standing on the holy ground of Calvary today, with eyes raised to the cross, we understand why the conscience of mankind for nineteen centuries has been drawn to this one scene as by a magnet, and why Christians have always felt that the heart of everything lies here. Jesus Himself knew and openly affirmed that by His death there would be let loose in the earth a saving, cleansing power beyond all calculation. That power has gone to work mainly along two lines.

On the one hand, the death of Jesus has *revealed sin in its true nature*. Let us remember that the evil things which put Jesus on the cross were by no means unfamiliar or abnormal. Self-interest in Caiaphas, fear in Pilate, impurity in Herod, anger and spite in the crowd—these were the things which, coming in contact with the Sinless One, deliberately compassed His death.

That is to say, Jesus was crucified by the ordinary sins of every day. We are all in this together. Our heart and conscience tell us, when we stand on Calvary, that what we see there is our own work, and that the sins we so lightly condone result always in the crucifixion of the Son of God. In this sense, to quote a great Christian conception, the Lamb is 'slain from the foundation of the world' (Rev. xiii, 8), and still is slain today. 'Jesus', said Pascal, 'will be in agony until the end of the world.'

> O break, O break, hard heart of mine
> Thy weak self-love and guilty pride
> His Pilate and His Judas were:
> Jesus, our Lord, is crucified!

So the cross of Jesus reveals the true nature and colour of sin, and by so doing creates saving penitence. This is one great secret of its power.

On the other hand, *it reveals God's almighty love*. Not to appease an angry God, not to induce Him to change His mind and love us, did Jesus die; any such idea is definitely unchristian. God's love is eternal and unchanging. There never was a time when God had to be persuaded to love. No, Calvary was not an inducement Jesus offered to God: it was God's own love in action. Just as from a volcano there flashes out now and again for one sudden, startling moment the elemental fire which burns unseen at the earth's heart, so at the cross of Jesus God's love leapt out in history, sheer flame, showing in that crowning moment of time what God is in His inmost being for ever. The cross reveals the heart of the eternal. It makes grace real. It makes love available for needy souls. It reconciles the sinful, and brings the world to God's feet.

20: THE TRIUMPH

Mon. 1 Cor. xv, 3-9
                    The Appearances of the Risen Lord
Tues. John xx, 11-18   Mary Magdalene at the Tomb
Wed. Luke xxiv, 13-35
                    The Christ of the Emmaus Road
Thur. John xx, 19-23   Behind Closed Doors
Fri. John xx, 24-31   The Faith of Thomas
Sat. John xxi, 1-14   By the Lake of Galilee
Sun. Acts ii, 29-36   The Resurrection Gospel

Hymnary 118: 'Christ the Lord is risen today'
    „   130: 'The golden gates are lifted up'

1. *The Defeat of Death*

Let us look at two pictures. One is an upper room in Jerusalem on the night after Calvary, and a little group of men cowering behind bolted and barricaded doors. Fear is on every face. But even more markedly than fear, dejection is written there, hopeless, final, irretrievable dejection. Dazed and stunned and bewildered they sit in silence, too heartbroken to speak, too benumbed in soul to pray. Everything is at an end. Fate has beaten them. There is nothing left to live for. That is the one picture—utter, abject defeat.

Here is the other. A few weeks later. The same group of men. But not skulking behind closed doors now! They are out in the streets. They are men aflame with superhuman confidence. Their words ring like iron. They have a message to which the world cannot but listen. They are absolutely fearless and overwhelmingly happy. They are planning the conquest of the earth.

Look first at the one picture and then at the other—there the misery of blasted hopes, here the valour of the saints; there a fumbling, futile remnant, here the nucleus of a marching, militant Church—and only the briefest span of time between. How had this startling, almost incredible change in these men's lives occurred? Can we explain it? Yes. Between the two pictures something had happened—*Christ was risen.*

Never did an enterprise look more utterly ruined than when Jesus of Nazareth was taken down from the cross and laid in the tomb. 'He was crucified, dead, and buried,' says our Apostles' Creed, and the very words seem burdened with an awful finality. If the disciples thought about the future at all, they saw themselves creeping back shame-facedly to the homes they had once left so eagerly at Jesus' bidding, and they heard in fancy the jeers and taunts of the village street as they so ingloriously returned. 'I go a fishing,' said Simon Peter, but he knew all too well that even if he took up again the old life where he had laid it down it could never content him now: his experience of Jesus had come in between, and that had spoilt him for anything else for ever. Not only was Christ dead: Christianity was dead. And against its tomb a great stone of despair had been rolled.

Yet it may have been that in one heart here and another there some dim thought may have hovered that what they had witnessed at Calvary was not and could not be the end. In John Masefield's drama, *The Trial of Jesus*, there is a striking passage in which Longinus, the Roman centurion in command of the soldiers at the cross, comes back to Pilate to hand in his report on the day's work. The report is given; and then Procula, Pilate's wife, beckons to the centurion and begs him to tell her how the prisoner died. And when the story has been told, 'Do you think He is dead?' she suddenly asks. 'No, lady,' answers Longinus, 'I don't.' 'Then where is He?' 'Let loose in the world, lady, where neither Roman nor Jew can stop His truth. Standing in the shadow of the cross where the cleanest, noblest soul who ever walked this earth hangs dying, we hear an inward voice telling us that that cannot be the end. It was not the end. In the great, simple words of the Creed, 'The third day

He rose again from the dead; He ascended into heaven, and sitteth on the right hand of God the Father Almighty.'

2. The Resurrection a Historic Fact

The evidence for the Resurrection is irrefragable. Divergences of detail may certainly be found in the various Gospel accounts of this supreme event. But these, so far from shaking and destroying the credibility of the narratives, actually enhance it. Think of the circumstances. Here were the disciples, caught up into a whirl of stupendous amazement and bewilderment by the discovery that their Lord was still alive. Here were the other eye-witnesses of the event—Mary Magdalene and others—living through a time of supreme emotion and excitement. Is it to be wondered at that when at a later day the Evangelists came to gather the memories of these crowded, glorious hours and to set them down in their Gospels, some differences of detail should have appeared? Does that detract in the smallest degree from the value of their evidence? On the contrary, we should have had far more reason to be uneasy if such differences had not been there. For then it would have been hard to resist the conclusion that the various accounts had been deliberately harmonized. A good illustration of the way in which such surface variations as we find here are bound to come into reports of stirring and exciting events is provided by the experience of the Great War: eyewitnesses of one particular incident would describe it each in his own way. The Gospel evidence for the Resurrection of Jesus bears the marks of reality and authenticity on the very face of it. It is the witness of men who were themselves utterly convinced, and from first to last it carries conviction.

It is a point of quite exceptional importance that when, just fifty days after the Crucifixion, the apostolic preaching of the Resurrection began in Jerusalem, *the evidence convinced thousands*. If the facts were not true which the apostles were openly declaring, and declaring with such startling results, then obviously now—when the alleged occurrence itself was so recent—now was the time for their enemies to challenge the facts and disprove them. There were people in Jerusalem who wanted nothing better than to see the new movement nipped in the bud, and we may be sure that if by any means the central theme of the apostolic message could have been discredited and proved to be false, they would have lost no time in doing it. But no such refutation of the apostles' case was forthcoming. Easy as it would obviously at that time have been, if Jesus in point of fact had never risen from the dead, to prove that He had not risen, no such proof was even attempted. This failure on the part of Jesus' enemies is itself first-rate evidence of the truth of what the apostles were declaring. The facts remained unchallenged because they were above challenge. The Resurrection Gospel was incontestable.

But quite apart from documentary evidence, a clear witness lies in *the amazing transformation of the disciples themselves*, to which reference has already been made. It takes the Resurrection, nothing less, to explain the sudden and complete change in these men from absolute despair and futility to absolute radiance and mastery of life. This is the rock on which any theory of an invented story or of a mere visionary fancy goes to pieces. The idea that the disciples, having lost their Master, fabricated a tale of His return to them, is negatived and made absurd by the lives of the men themselves. Inventions do not transform characters, nor do men endure martyrdom for impostures. And every attempt which has ever been made to explain the disciples' belief on a purely visionary basis has ended by raising far more problems than it solved. One thing, and one thing alone, makes what happened to these eleven men credible—Christ was risen indeed.

The evidence, however, goes beyond the original disciples, it includes *the fact of the Christian Church*. It is a simple fact of history that it was the Resurrection belief that brought the Church into being; and when the Church swept out from Jerusalem to the conquest of the earth, it was the Resurrection message that was the driving-power. The truth of the amazing facts with which the closing chapters of our four

Gospels deal is witnessed to by the whole course of Christian history for nineteen centuries; for no one seriously believes that a spiritual movement like the Church, so indestructible in its nature, so illimitable in its possibilities, so indispensable in its value for the souls of men, could ever have sprung from, or been inspired by, anything which was not utterly and genuinely real. If Christ had not verily risen, the Church which bears His name would have perished long ago, for fierce attacks, social, political, intellectual, have been launched against it down the years. Many a time, indeed, it has seemed doomed and dead, and the gravediggers—Hume, Voltaire, and others—have been busy at its tomb; but always it has broken the grave, and rolled the stone away. Only the fact of the Resurrection of Jesus can explain the Church of the living God.

All these lines of evidence are valid and of great importance. But the supreme proof of the Resurrection, the thing which makes it not only credible but inevitable, is *the person of Jesus Himself*. Now this is what the disciples, after the first startling shock had given place to steady certitude, came to see. Jesus being who and what Jesus was, anything other than that He should rise again was unthinkable. As one of themselves, on reflection, expressed it, 'It was not possible that He should be holden of death' (Acts ii, 24). That was a great conviction, and our study of the life of Jesus with His disciples must have disclosed some of the factors that entered into it.

One thing which had always impressed these men about their Master was *His sheer vitality*. 'In Him was life,' says John (John i, 4). 'The Prince of Life', Peter calls Him (Acts iii, 15). Open your Gospels at any page, and the first thing which strikes you is that here is Someone as radiant as the face of the morning, as vital as the breath of God. Everyone who came in contact with Jesus felt that He had enormous reserves at His command, and that however much they saw in Him there was always more behind. This explains the astounding daring of the requests they brought to Him. Leprosy, for instance, was notoriously incurable; but 'Lord, if Thou wilt,' said the leper simply, 'Thou canst make me clean' (Matt. viii. 2). They could not conceive any situation for which Christ would not be adequate. Even death would have to give way.

Moreover, there was *the love of Jesus*. From the first day His disciples had known Him, that love had had the stamp of deathlessness upon it. It had flooded their whole world with a light which never was on sea or land. Such a love could never be robbed of its object. It would break the tomb, to stand beside its own.

But even more important was *the sinlessness, the moral perfection, of Jesus*. We have seen already, in our study of the healing miracles of Jesus, how intimately the Master's mighty works were bound up with, and dependent upon, the fact of His own sinlessness (p. 99). In Jesus, alone amongst the sons of men, the final break with sin had been achieved; and the power of spirit over matter, which in others was blocked and thwarted at every turn by sin's taint and bias, was in Him fully set free. Mighty works thus flowed naturally from Jesus, and the Resurrection, the mightiest of all, ceased to be impossible or even improbable, and became inevitable.

The decisive thing for these disciples was *their personal experience of Jesus*. Daily fellowship with Him had taught them that He was more than man; and though Calvary momentarily dimmed and clouded that high faith, it shone out clear again. Having come to feel towards Jesus as they had always felt towards God, they saw now that the Resurrection had been certain from the first: for if Jesus died, and that were all, then God Himself would die. So in the last resort, the proof of the Resurrection is the person of Jesus Himself and men's experience of Jesus. It was not possible that He—God incarnate—should be holden of death.

3. *The Master Reunited with His Friends*

We turn now from the fact of the Resurrection to the re-corded appearances of the Risen One. The first to see Jesus after His death was Mary Magdalene (John xx, 1, 11; cf. Matt. xxviii, 1, 9). The greatest news that ever broke upon the world, the news which was to change the whole life of humanity and shake down thrones and revolutionize kingdoms, the news which still today girdles the earth with everlasting hope and sends a new thrill through every Christian soul on Easter morning, was given first to one humble, obscure woman out of whom seven devils had gone, who had nothing to distinguish her but her forgiven heart, and no claim at all but her love. Mary had come out, before dawn was in the sky, to sit beside a dead body. She was telling herself that everything else but that was gone—the voice of Jesus that would never speak again, the light in those eyes that would shine no more, the living soul that was fled for ever—all gone, and only the dead body left for love and gratitude to cling to and try to serve. She came, and even that was gone. This was her moment of final desolation. 'They have taken away my Lord, and I know not where they have laid Him.' Blinded with tears, her eyes could not recognize someone standing near, but He called her by her name, and then she knew. 'Jesus saith unto her, Mary. She turned herself, and saith unto Him, Rabboni; which is to say, Master.' What she had once been saved from and forgiven was the measure of her devotion; and always it is those who love Jesus best, who see Him first.

St. Luke records the beautiful story of the Christ of the Emmaus road (Luke xxiv, 13 ff). Of all possible disappointments in life, to be disappointed in Jesus Christ must surely be the worst: and that was the disappointment which was burdening the hearts of Cleopas and his friend as they journeyed home in the falling twilight. Brokenly they spoke to each other of the hope that was gone, and memories of happier days came crowding in—days when, looking at Jesus, so young and strong and steady-eyed and godlike, they had been sure that this was the coming King and the Captain of ten thousand souls: 'We trusted that it had been He which should have redeemed Israel.' And now it had all ended in disillusionment and heartache and regret. But Christ is often nearest when men think Him gone for ever, and as they listened to the talk of the stranger who had joined them on the way their hearts began to burn. Almost before they knew it, they had reached their journey's end: never surely had the Jerusalem to Emmaus road been so short as on that night. It was hard to say good-bye to the stranger whose company had so mysteriously charmed their gloom away and brought cheerfulness breaking in, and something guided them to keep Him with them a little longer and to invite Him to their table. There something happened—was it some familiar gesture as He broke the bread? Or was it the grace He said over the simple meal? Or was it the hands in which He raised the bread, hands marked with nails? Whatever it was, it rent the veil which had been hanging before their eyes, and they knew Him, and called Him by His name.

That same night in Jerusalem the lost and leaderless disciples were reunited with their Master. 'When the doors were shut . . . came Jesus, and stood in the midst' (John xx, 19; cf. Luke xxiv, 36). Two of the disciples were missing in that great hour—Judas and Thomas. Judas, in the restrained and solemn language of the Book of Acts, had gone 'to his own place' (Acts i, 25). But where was Thomas? Doubtless he was wandering alone in the dark, brooding on his own deep grief, and unable to bear any company now, not even the company of his fellow-disciples. He may even have been haunting the deserted slopes of Calvary. Next morning when Peter and John, with a strange new light on their faces, accosted him and shared with him their wonderful tidings, he looked at them sadly and told them they were deluded. But a week later he was in the upper room; and Jesus, who is always so patient with honest doubt, came again. This time the Master's self-revelation was specifically adapted to His one groping follower's need. Thomas now saw what the others had already seen, and entered into their experience; and with a great cry, 'My Lord and my God', he swept the midnight from his soul.

Reading the Evangelists' narratives of the appearances of the Risen Lord, we are struck by this notable fact, that while the Jesus whom these men and women saw was certainly the same dear Master whom they had known in bygone days, there was none the less a difference. There was a certain reserve about Him now. 'Touch Me not,' He said (John xx, 17). It could not be called aloofness, but at least it meant that one chapter in the book of their fellowship together was now closed, and another chapter, a higher order of fellowship, beginning. Ordinary limitations of space and time had ceased to hold Him: He came to them, and went in ways they could not understand (Luke xxiv, 36; John xx, 19). Recognition did not always happen immediately, as we have seen already in the stories of Mary in the garden and the Emmaus travellers. 'When they saw Him, some doubted' (Matt. xxviii, 17). 'He appeared in another form' (Mark xvi, 12). 'They supposed that they had seen a spirit' (Luke xxiv, 37). 'Jesus stood on the shore: but the disciples knew not that it was Jesus' (John xxi, 4). He was the same —yet different. He was still the friend with whom in former days they had walked through the cornfields of Galilee and bivouacked at night beneath the open sky, the Master who had taught them such memorable lessons from the lilies of the field and the birds of the air, from yokes and ploughs and candlelight and the children shouting at their games: yet somehow they were conscious of a change. But that, as they came to understand, was only to be expected. For He had been on a long journey since Calvary had snatched Him from them. He had returned from the undiscovered country from whose bourne no traveller (it was thought) could ever return. And the breath of that other country was all about Him. He belonged no longer to this narrow, material world, with its time and space restrictions: He belonged to that ampler, higher world of spirit which alone is real and eternal.

4. *The Inner Meaning of the Resurrection*

We have dwelt in this study upon the fact of the Resurrection, and upon those recorded appearances by which the fact was first heralded. We turn now finally to the inner meaning of the fact. It is obvious that an event like this must have had consequences, not only for the disciples, or even for the Church, but for the whole world. What did the Resurrection of Jesus mean?

It meant, first, God's vindication of His Son. When the disciples went out preaching and proclaiming their Risen Lord, they used significantly the passive, not the active voice, to describe the event; they said regularly, not 'He rose,' but 'He was raised,' for with deep spiritual insight they saw that what had happened had been nothing less than God in action, God's right arm made bare on behalf of His beloved Son (Acts ii, 24, 32; iii, 15; iv, 10; Rom. vi, 4, 9; 1 Cor. xv, 15). That one who had died a felon's death should nevertheless be Messiah was an idea not only shocking but actually blasphemous to orthodox Jewish minds, and many devout people who had secret hopes about Jesus must have considered that the cross finished His pretensions. But here in the Resurrection was God's sudden, unexpected attestation of the very highest and most daring hopes that had ever been cherished about Jesus, God's own seal set convincingly to Jesus' Messianic claim, God's final vindication of His Son.

It meant, further, the vindication of righteousness. Daringly and gallantly Jesus had staked everything He had and was upon the absolute validity of goodness and truth and love. These were the things whose supremacy He had always preached: for these He had consecrated His own life up to the last limit of self-consecration; and for His belief in these He was ready at last to die. Had the sinless Jesus remained in the tomb, the conclusion would have been irresistible that this world is a moral chaos, and goodness a poor mirage, and honour a mischievous delusion. But on the Resurrection morning it was just as if the whole nature of things by one mighty act had endorsed and countersigned the noble, unselfish way of living. We know now that the universe itself is on the side of the man who fights the good fight. Jesus rose: and righteousness was vindicated.

The Resurrection meant also the assurance of immortality. Pagans, watching Christ's men at work in the world, were struck by many things, but by nothing more forcibly than the Christians' contempt of death: and it was the Risen Christ who had robbed the king of terrors of his power. 'I go to prepare a place for you,' He had said, 'and I will come again and receive you unto Myself' (John xiv, 2, 3); and if death meant that, what room was there for fear? The Master's conquest of death involved theirs. 'Because I live, ye shall live also' (John xiv, 19). Easter morning brought immortality to light; and the Christians, seeing death lying broken, could say with the Psalmist, 'God is gone up with a shout, the Lord with the sound of a trumpet' (Ps. xlvii, 5).

Finally, the Resurrection meant a Christ alive for evermore. Even when the forty wonderful days succeeding the first Easter were over and Jesus' visible presence was withdrawn, the disciples knew they had not lost Him. Every day His own word was being verified in their experience—'Lo, I am with you alway, even unto the end' (Matt. xxviii, 20). Through all the vicissitudes of their active service, it was no fading memory that sustained them, but a living presence and a daily comradeship; and when, like their Master before them, they saw death coming to meet them violently, it was His hands that held them up. Nor was their experience unique. Hosts of men and women since the disciples' day have walked and talked with Christ. This is no miracle. For if Christ is risen indeed, which means if He is living now, what is more natural than that His own friends should sometimes meet Him face to face? Such fellowship is a direct consequence of the Resurrection. There was a day when Matthew Arnold, looking out upon the world, found himself crying:

> Oh, had I lived in that great day,
>   How had its glory new
> Fill'd earth and heaven, and caught away
>   My ravish'd spirit too! . . .
> Now he is dead! Far hence he lies
>   In the lorn Syrian town;
> And on his grave, with shining eyes,
>   The Syrian stars look down.

No. Arnold was wrong. He was utterly and finally wrong.

Why seek the living among the dead? Christ is alive! The late Dr Dale, the great preacher of Birmingham, described how one day, while he was writing an Easter sermon, the fact of the Resurrection broke in upon him as it had never done before. ' "Christ is alive." I said to myself: "alive!" and then I paused:—"alive!" and then I paused again; "alive! Can that really be true? living as really as I myself am?" I got up and walked about repeating, "Christ is living! Christ is living!" At first it seemed strange and hardly true, but at last it came upon me as a burst of sudden glory.'

Yes, Christ is alive. To thousands upon thousands at the present hour this is no mere theory or vague, uncertain rumour, but proved, inviolable experience; and if they are facing life victoriously now where once they were defeated, it is because they have found the same Risen Lord who walked among the flowers of the garden on the morning of the first Easter day.

21: MASTER AND LORD OF LIFE

Hymnary 155: 'Mine eyes have seen the glory of the
coming of the Lord'
   „   497: 'Just as I am, Thine own to be'

[*Note to Teacher.*—As some members of the class will probably be
contemplating coming into the full communion of the Church by
profession of faith, it will be well if the teacher takes the opportunity
provided by this closing lesson of showing how Christ's personal
challenge and His claim for a full self-surrender are linked up with
membership in His Church. Christ's challenge and claim should have
been felt, directly and indirectly, through all the lessons of the course;
but here the teacher should present them in their most pointed form.
And the last meeting of this class ought to lead on quite naturally to
the first meeting of a young communicants' class.]

1. *Christ's Finished and Unfinished Work*

We have come now to the end of the story. But the end of
the story of Christ is a beginning. The four Evangelists to
whom we owe the story were fully conscious of this, and it
never occurred to them to write *Finis* when the last page
was complete. As each of them laid down his pen and closed
his book he felt that what he had written was only volume
one, the first instalment of a story which still was being
enacted and was destined to continue through unborn
generations and ages without number. One of them—St.
Luke—at a later time took up his pen again to give the world
volume two; and he prefaced this second instalment of the
story of Christ—*The Acts of the Apostles*, he called it—with a

reference to his original book: 'The former treatise have I made of all that Jesus *began* both to do and teach' (Acts i, 1); for Luke saw that however much of the story he had told, there was vastly more to follow. In a sense, of course, the task of Jesus on this earth was finished when He returned to His Father.

> 'All His work is ended,'
> Joyfully we sing:
> 'Jesus hath ascended!
> Glory to our King!'

'Christ, being raised from the dead,' said St. Paul, 'dieth no more' (Rom. vi, 9). All that was over. The earthly ministry, the agony of Gethsemane, the arrest and trial, the weariness of the Via Dolorosa, the death on the cross—all that was finished, and would never happen again. These were historic events. They came, and passed. They happened once, and only once. The full price of sin was paid. The revelation of redeeming love was perfect and complete. Nothing was left undone. Nothing remains to be added. Beyond Jesus we need never hope to go. In this sense, at any rate, it is true that the story of Jesus finds at Calvary and the empty tomb and the Ascension its culmination and completion and crown. True—but not the whole truth. For while the Gospel is securely and solidly rooted in history, with its roots firmly twined round the unshakable rock of historic fact, the Christ of the Gospel is more than a mere figure of history. It was no historic reminiscence which got hold of Saul of Tarsus outside Damascus, and flung him violently to the ground from his horse, and revolutionized his life. It was no old, remembered story which sent the Christian message flaming like a prairie fire across the earth. It was something more than the recollection of a noble example which made men glow as the men of Pentecost glowed, and sing as the Franciscans sang, and die as the Covenanters died. The fact of the matter is that the first volume of the life of Christ, the evangelic record, has been followed by a hundred others; and one is actually being written at the present hour wherever down the crowded streets of life the Master moves, seeking and finding the lost, binding up the broken-hearted, and driving out devils in the name of the Lord God Almighty. The story had not ended when Calvary and Easter were past. It had only just begun.

The first disciples realized this very clearly. Knowing Jesus as they now knew Him, they could not conceive any lower place for Him than the throne of the whole earth. Jesus, they saw, must be Master and Lord of life. So they dedicated themselves to the magnificent, amazing adventure which was to carry the cross in less than three hundred years from the ignominy of Golgotha to the throne of the Caesars. On the face of it, it seemed impossible that these few men, with no weapons to wield save one, the weapon of love, should make any impression on a world that had the weapon of force and was determined to use it. It seemed impossible that they should stand up against the vested interests of materialism and secularism, the 'principalities and powers' of which Paul spoke, and the entrenched selfishness of the world. When they first set out, with their unheard-of-dream looking out at their eyes, the world simply laughed them to scorn. And when in spite of laughter and scorn they kept going on, marching indomitably from town to town and land to land until they were knocking at the gates of Rome, the world began to take them seriously and tried to bar their way. But by this time blazing fire and torturing rack and furious insult were all in vain. The dream prevailed, and the world was at their feet. It was not their own achievement, they always said, but Christ's. It was the life-story, whose first volume contained Bethlehem and Galilee and Calvary, being continued. It was still Christ in action, Christ going from strength to strength, Christ alive and working in the earth.

And they were right. Nothing but the life of Christ in these men can explain the power they evidenced. On various levels that power made itself felt. It was power *on the physical level*. New and exhilarating energies were liberated in their very bodies, enabling them to carry through with zest and verve things which to other men would have been impossible. It was power *on the mental level*. Ill-educated and illiterate many of these early followers of Christ may have been; but something had happened to them which gave them a power of initiative, a grasp of essentials, and a directness of decision the like of which the world had never seen before. It was power *on the moral level*. Some of them had been rescued from devouring and devastating passions; some had to fight hot, stubborn temptations; some had to live in cities that were dens of corruption; and yet spotless and white-robed and uncorrupted they kept the narrow way, clean with the very cleanness of Jesus. It was power *on the spiritual level*. Wherever they went, other lives were changed and souls redeemed, and mighty miracles of grace were witnessed. Never for a moment did they dream of claiming for themselves the credit of all this power. Their explanation of it was at once incredibly simple and incredibly daring. It was Christ in them. It was a new Gospel being written. It was a new, wonderful stage in the story of their Master's life. And because of that, they knew that nothing could ever frustrate them or bring their adventure to defeat.

March we forth in the strength of God, with the banner of Christ unfurled,
That the light of the glorious Gospel of truth may shine throughout the world:
Fight we the fight with sorrow and sin, to set their captives free,
That the earth may be filled with the glory of God, as the waters cover the sea.

2. *The Passion to Make Christ King*

Four things drove the early disciples out into the world to witness to Jesus as Lord and Master, four things which still in the altered circumstances of today lay the duty of witness upon every true disciple.

First, there was *the command of Jesus Himself*. 'All power is given unto Me in heaven and in earth. Go ye therefore, and teach all nations' (Matt. xxviii, 18 f). This world outlook had indeed characterized the life and teaching of Jesus from the first (e.g. Matt. v, 14; viii, 11; xxiv, 14; xxvi, 13); but with this clear and definite command now ringing in their ears, the disciples could not doubt what their Lord required of them. St. Luke records the fact that when Jesus gave His followers their commission, He added the words, 'beginning at Jerusalem' (Luke xxiv, 47). That is an interesting touch, suggesting that a man's witness to Christ is to start right on the very spot where he happens to be. Jerusalem had been the scene of the disciples' failure and shameful desertion of their Master in His hour of need; in the same place, they were now to give their witness and stand up for Him before the eyes of all men. And was it not wonderfully in keeping with the love and patience and forgiving spirit which they had always seen in Jesus that the city which had killed Him should, by His own decree, be the first to receive their Gospel? But the message, starting there, was to be carried across the world. This was their Lord's command; and they knew that on their obedience to it their very fellowship with Him would depend.

All Christian service in the world has that command behind it. Christ does not ask His friends as a favour to bear witness to Him among men: He claims it as a duty. 'Ye are My friends, if ye do whatsoever I command you' (John xv, 14). Christianity does not mean complimenting Christ as genius, or artist, or teacher: it means bowing to Christ as Commander. 'When ye shall have done all those things which are commanded you, say, We are unprofitable servants: we have done that which was our duty to do' (Luke xvii, 10). And when people say, as they sometimes do, that they can see no reason why the Church of Christ should go crusading at the ends of the earth while there is still so much to do at home and so many untaken forts in the rear of Christ's advance, the answer must be, not only that it is the very death of religion when it is not propagating itself and scattering itself abroad, but also that they are mistaken in imagining that this is in any sense an open question. It is emphatically not an open question. The great command settled it once for all. And the man who still debates and argues it is daring to correct Jesus Christ. That wrecks his position. The Master's ruling has been given; and He means it to be obeyed.

The second thing which sent the disciples out to witness in the world was *the urgency of the situation*. They were convinced that the end of the world was at hand. It might happen in their own lifetime. Had not Jesus assured them that some would not taste death till they had seen the Son of man coming in His Kingdom (Matt. xvi, 28)? Were His own words not written on their hearts—'Verily I say unto you, that this generation shall not pass, till all these things be done' (Mark xiii, 30)? Clearly no time must be lost if the evangelization of the world was to be achieved before the end came. 'The Gospel must first be published among all nations' (Mark xiii, 10). The King's business required haste, for the heedless world was perishing. Everywhere men were sitting in darkness and the shadow of death, hopeless and godless and lost and ruined: and the end was hurrying on. Christ's men were driven forth to preach by the sheer urgency of the situation.

This, too, lays the duty of witness upon their successors today. One startling factor in the present world situation is the breakdown among masses of men of ancient systems of belief and conduct, which has left them without guiding principles of any kind—like ships on stormy seas, without rudder or compass; and it is not speaking in any alarmist fashion to say that unless we can confront that situation with Christ, it may in the long run overwhelm us and lead the world back to chaos. This is a day when every man who has been with Jesus, and believes in Jesus, ought to feel himself called, by the very urgency of the situation, to be a living witness to Jesus in the world.

The third thing which drove the disciples out was *the glory of the message*. They had found something the like of which had never burst upon the world before. There was the wonder of forgiveness, for instance. Other religions were, no doubt, ready to tell men who had sinned of a way by which, with hard, painful effort, they might creep slowly back to decency again; but Christ's religion spoke of God's arms round the raggedest, muddiest soul. Or think of death, through fear of which mankind had always been subject to

bondage: here were men who could laugh in death's grim
face, for Christ had conquered. Moreover, God, in the
thoughts of half the world, was a jealous, threatening, implacable tyrant: but Christ's men knew—and it thrilled their
hearts with joy unspeakable to know it—that God was love
and nothing but love, and love for evermore. They had
found a reality beyond the world's furthest dreams, and it
was the glory of the message that drove them forth and sent
them flaming round the earth.

'They who have the torch', says an old Greek proverb,
'must pass on the light'; and every disciple today who has
once grasped the truth that the Gospel which he professes
is far and away the most glorious thing which ever entered
the heart of man, is bound to be a herald. As Temple Gairdner of Cairo put it, 'The true appeal for missions is that if
Christ prayed those prayers (the prayers of Gethsemane and
Calvary), then of course the world must know.' At the heart
of the Christian message stands the magnificent, magnetic,
adorable figure of Jesus Christ Himself; and the very glory
of that message must constrain our witness.

The fourth thing which sent the disciples out (and this
really included all the others) was the conviction which they
embodied in the earliest Christian creed—*Jesus is Lord*. The
very first Christian sermon which was ever preached culminated with the words, 'God hath made that same Jesus,
whom ye have crucified, both Lord and Christ' (Acts ii, 36);
and it was this Lordship of Jesus that was the heart of everything. In Paul's statement, 'We preach Christ Jesus as Lord'
(2 Cor. iv, 5), the theme of all the early preaching is sum-
marized; and the simple confession 'Jesus is Lord' was the
sole creed of the earliest days (Rom. x, 9; 1 Cor. xii, 3; Acts
x, 36). Nineteen centuries of Christianity have made this
title familiar, and perhaps have dulled its wonder for us.
But when the first disciples, borrowing from their Old
Testament the very word which the Greek version had used
to translate the Hebrew Jehovah, took this name and
applied it to the Master with whom they had walked the
roads of Galilee, it was a mighty achievement of faith. By

this title they meant that the friend to whom they owed so much was one day to be Judge of all mankind. The voice whose every accent they knew and loved would yet awaken the whole earth like a trumpet. All the kingdoms of the world would be His, and He would be Lord indeed. Despised and rejected of men these disciples often might be, as their Master had been before them; but through it all, they kept dreaming their dreams, envisaging for their Leader an empire greater than anything that ever swam into Caesar's ken, and planning for Him a world strategy compared with which all the campaigns of an Alexander were a mere nothing. When groups of them met together in that hostile, contemptuous world, 'He is Lord of all,' they whispered; and their password was 'Maranatha', 'Lord, come!' (1 Cor. xvi, 22; cf. Rev. xxii, 20).

Far simpler than any subsequent confession of faith which men have arrived at, the creed 'Jesus is Lord' is nevertheless profound in its meaning and world-shaking in its consequences. To apply it faithfully involves asserting the absolute sovereignty of Jesus over every department of one's own life first, and then over all the life of the world. It means the throne of the universe for Christ. It is still a daring claim, as it was at the first; but no one who has honestly faced the fact of Christ can have any doubt at all that that throne is His by right. It has been bought with a price—bought with the hunger in the desert when He would not make the stones into bread; bought with the tears He shed over the sins of men; bought with the sweat of Gethsemane which was like great drops of blood; bought with the bitter cross where they broke his body in death; bought with the deathless love which through all the years has refused resolutely to let a lost world go. The Captain of the hosts of humanity has Himself been in the ranks. He has experienced the hardship and peril of life's campaign from the common soldier's side of it. He has endured the discipline. If He rides at the head of the host today, it is because He once marched on foot. If one day He is to be King over all the sons of men, it is because at the first He was not ashamed to call us brethren. 'Wherefore,' says Paul finely, summing up in that word the whole story of Jesus' sufferings and sorrows, 'wherefore God also hath highly exalted Him, and given Him a name which is above every name, that at the name of Jesus every knee should bow' (Phil. ii, 9). Yes, Christ's sovereign rights have been bought with a price. This is He who came out of great tribulation: therefore is He upon the throne. And our own conscience bears witness that that is His due place. Like the centurion of Capernaum (Matt. viii, 9) who felt instinctively that Jesus had 'soldiers under Him', unseen powers to do His bidding, and that behind Him was all the weight and majesty of empire, so we feel and know, with everything that is deepest and truest within us, that His Kingdom cannot fail, and that one day the whole universe of earth and heaven shall acknowledge Him alone.

3. Jesus Shall Reign

That day has not yet dawned. But slowly and steadily it is coming nearer. Already one Figure can be seen standing where the roads of life meet. *Jesus is standing where the roads of nationality meet.* High up amongst the Andes Mountains where the lands of Chile and the Argentine touch, there stands a great bronze statue of Christ, forged out of the metal of discarded guns; and on the base of the statue the words are engraved: 'Sooner shall these mountains crumble into dust than Argentines and Chileans break the peace they have sworn to maintain at the feet of Christ the Redeemer.' *Jesus is standing where the roads of class meet.* General Booth of the Salvation Army used to insist that no man's arms were long enough to reach out and give a hand to rich and poor at once: human arms may not do it, but the arms which were stretched wide on Calvary can. *Jesus is standing where the roads of literature meet.* The world's literature for nineteen hundred years has been haunted by Jesus, haunted by His bleeding hands and feet, and by His burning eyes. Those two giants of British and American literature, Carlyle and Emerson, once met at Carlyle's Scottish home; and as they walked together over the hill, discussing all things in heaven and earth, the little village church came into view beneath them, and Carlyle stopped. Turning to Emerson, he said,' Christ died on the tree; that built Dunscore Kirk yonder; that brought you and me together. Time has only a relative existence.' *Jesus is standing where the roads of religion meet.* Just before the World Missionary Conference in Jerusalem in 1928 an exhaustive and comprehensive survey was carried through of all the great non-Christian faiths. What was the result? In the words of Dr John Mott: 'It was overwhelmingly proved that the more open-minded, honest, just, and generous we were in dealing with the non-Christian faiths, the higher Christ loomed in His absolute uniqueness, sufficiency, supremacy, and universality.' 'There is no one else', said a prominent Hindu to Stanley Jones, 'who is seriously bidding for the heart of the world except Jesus Christ. There is no one else on the field.' Already one Figure is standing where the roads of all the ages meet; and to those who have once seen Him, and experienced in their own lives His power, this above all else is certain, that a day is drawing near when every gate in the universe will be lifting up its head to let the King come in.

All this is true; and because it is true, one question leaps out on us from every page of the story of Jesus, one challenge which no soul can finally avoid: Is He Master and Lord of *my* life? Every year, thousands of young people enter the Church by profession of faith. That is to say, every year they stand up in public and take upon themselves a vow that they are going to make Christ Lord of all. Think what would happen if that multitude were witnessing for Christ with all their might! Think what would happen if our own lives were really His, with no 'ifs' and 'buts' and conditions and reservations, but His up to the very hilt. Think what it would mean for ourselves. Think what it would mean for the world around us. And think what it would mean for Christ.

> O that, with yonder sacred throng,
>   We at His feet may fall,
> Join in the everlasting song,
>   And crown Him Lord of all!